BY ROBERT ARDREY

The Hunting Hypothesis

ROBERT ARDREY

The Hunting Hypothesis

A Personal Conclusion Concerning the Evolutionary Nature of Man

NEW YORK   ATHENEUM

1976

Chapter 8, "Interglacial Man", originally appeared in Playboy magazine.

Library of Congress Cataloging in Publication Data

Ardrey, Robert.   The hunting hypothesis
Bibliography: p.   Includes index.
1. Man—Animal nature.   2. Human evolution.
3. Aggressiveness (Psychology)   I. Title.
GN280.7.A72   1976   573.2   75-37781

ISBN 0-689-10672-6

To Raymond Arthur Dart

While we are members of the intelligent primate family, we are uniquely human even in the noblest sense, because for untold millions of years we alone killed for a living.

Contents

The Hunting Hypothesis

The Hunting Hypothesis

Why is man man?

As long as we have had minds to think with, stars to ponder upon, dreams to disturb us, curiosity to inspire us, hours free for meditation, words to place our thoughts in order, the question like a restless ghost has prowled the cellars of our consciousness.

Why is man man? What forces divine or mundane delivered to our natural world that remarkable creature, the human being? No literate, civilized people or illiterate primitive tribe has failed to heed the ghost. The question inhabits us all, as universal in our species as the capacity for speech. Did we enter this world carried out of some primal forest on the back of a sacred elephant? Were we coughed up on a pebbly shore by a benevolent, immaculate fish? How frequently, in our oldest myths, the animal participated in the Creation. Even the garden called Eden had its snake.

Our primitive perceptions of the contribution of the animal to the human presence have been confirmed by the sciences. But the sciences have not revealed why a sapient species should consistently have been attracted by those explanations of our nature that make a minimum of sense. Even the thoughtful Greeks rejected the quite sensible suggestion of an early thinker, Xenophanes, that if cattle had hands and could paint, they would paint their gods in the likeness of cattle. It was too much for the Greeks, who promptly shelved Xenophanes.

3

Perhaps it is a portion of the human paradox that we apply our immense capacities for observation and logic to everything but ourselves. The American geneticist Theodosius Dobzhansky has defined those three traits distinguishing the human being as our capacity to communicate, our awareness of death, and our awareness of self. Few would strenuously disagree. Yet what Dobzhansky does not add is a capacity for misunderstanding which rivals our capacity to communicate; an awareness of death which has remained at a virtual standstill since Cro-Magnon man began painting his dead with red ocher some thirty thousand years ago; and a self-awareness which, despite or because of our hopes and our fears, has become in modern times more and more closely synonymous with self-delusion.

Not in our powers but in our paradoxes shall we search for the essence of man. There is little that lacks logic in the life of the rhesus monkey or the English robin or the Canadian beaver or, so far as we can judge, the extinct woolly rhinoceros. All make sense; it is *Homo sapiens* that does not. And perhaps that is why our sciences have so conspicuously failed, despite all their tools and their dedication, to advance very far our knowledge of ourselves. As nature abhors a vacuum, so science fails to enjoy the inconsistent.

Our approach to an understanding of man for many a recent decade has been to reduce him in size. I am reminded sometimes of the little old lady who lived by the road with a barn full of boxes of various shapes and dimensions. When a traveler stopped by her cottage, she would feed him kindly, then stuff him away in a box. But should he be of a size that fitted none of her boxes, then she would stuff all she could in the nearest-sized box and chop off the rest of him.

So has it been that so many trends in human estimate have been directed toward reducing man. We become creatures shaped by the various forces encountered in our lifetime. We become products, like cornflakes or Chevrolets. We are products of our culture, of traditional sanctions and rewards, of social environments that through privileges or deprivations have made us what we are. Even our sexuality, we are informed, is a role we have learned through appropriate toys, games, social attitudes. And whatever environmental influences have created us, we as individuals have contributed no more to our fates than has the inbred, undifferentiated laboratory rat as, searching for a food pellet, he avoids his electric shock.

The trend is not new. Karl Marx was no enemy of the natural sciences, yet his view of human beings as economic units came so to invest both his followers and his enemies that material determination became the centerpiece of socialism and capitalism alike. In similar fashion Sigmund Freud looked deeply into the animal world—or what was known of it at the turn of the century. Yet somehow his sexual principle, to an alarming degree in the work of his followers, became the single key with which to unlock the secret places of our nature. Perhaps the true fault lay in quite another trend that captured the sciences in later decades: the proposition that what you cannot measure does not exist.

Without doubt it was the easy way. Avoid the human reality. Take the yardstick of your choice and fit the human being to your measure. Speak always with respect of the dignity of man, while you reduce him to cornflakes. Do your tidy sums in human arithmetic; construct your logical boxes. And if an Einstein passes by, or a Rembrandt or a Shakespeare or a Darwin, any of whom surpasses your arithmetic, then it cannot be the fault of your box. Stuff him away somewhere and chop off what's left. We did it to Freud. We did it even to Marx.

So when we ask the question, Why is man man? the easy answer is to reduce him. But there is another way, and that is to denigrate him. Toward the close of *African Genesis* I wrote:

> Had man been born of a fallen angel, then the contemporary predicament would lie as far beyond solution as it would lie beyond explanation. Our wars and our atrocities, our crimes and our quarrels, our tyrannies and our injustices could be ascribed to nothing other than singular human achievement. And we should be left with a clear-cut portrait of man as a degenerate being endowed at birth with virtue's treasury whose only notable talent had been to squander it. But we were born of risen apes, not fallen angels, and the apes were armed killers besides. And so what shall we wonder at? Our murders and massacres and missiles, and our irreconcilable regiments? Or our treaties whatever they may be worth; our symphonies however seldom they may be played; our peaceful acres however frequently they may be converted into battlefields; our dreams however rarely they may be accomplished? The miracle of man is not how far he has sunk but how magnificently he has risen. We are known among the stars by our poems, not our corpses.

Much has happened in the sciences since I published those lines, for it has been a time of discovery and controversy. Just as in the time of Darwin himself, the evolutionist has been drawn, quartered, boiled in oil, burned at blithe stakes. We are pessimists; we endanger the human future. Yet I can today no more discover pessimism in those lines than I could when I wrote them in 1961.

Man is a marvel—yet not so marvelous as to demand miraculous explanation. Man is a mystery transcending all our arithmetic, and will remain so, I have little doubt, whatever the revelations of our future sciences. We may enter that mystery, however, gain a sense of its dimensions and its

6

grandeur, even come on a clue to its origins, but we shall never dispel it. Man as a species is far too ancient, far too varied, and as an animal far too complex, to submit to individual comprehension. We shall never make even an entrance to the mystery if we do not accept man as a paradox.

What is it to be a human being? We may say, to possess a capacity for learning beyond that of any other animal. We must add, however, if we are not to ignore our history, a frequent refusal to learn from experience that would shame a baboon. We may inspect our uniquely human foresight, the envy of any ape, yet wonder, Where was that foresight on the eve of our more suicidal undertakings? Might not the ape have known better?

Classic is our daring, classic our cowardice. Classic is our cruelty, classic our charity. No human inventory can fail to include our propensity for premeditated, organized murder of our fellows yet fail to note that an army is a model of co-operation and self-sacrifice, or that no other species so carefully, tenderly cares for its wounded, even for its enemies. Compassion and mercy lie deep in our nature, as deep perhaps as our callousness and indifference.

Altruism presents no problem for those who believe, with Jean-Jacques Rousseau, that man in his primal state was born happy, amiable, good. It presents a plant of thorns for the Darwinian, as we shall see. Yet apparent altruism is as much an ingredient of the human paradox as implacable dedication to self-interest. Those saints and martyrs in our past who carried their supposed consecration to the common good beyond death's threshold treasured at the same time a deathless hostility for the consecrations of others.

We obey; we rebel. And yesterday's rebel may be today's sheep as he follows the bell of a new authority's resonance. With overwhelming enthusiasm we may cooperate in the pursuit of a common goal, while tomorrow we fall into dissension, jealousy, and the dark delights of suspicion.

7

We are as different as our fingerprints. Sir Julian Huxley wrote that man is the most diverse of all wild species. (How frequently even responsible scientists forget that we are not domesticated, that we are not, like the dog or the cow, a product of controlled breeding, but are merely tamed.) Another great English biologist, the geneticist J. B. S. Haldane, characterized the evolutionary potential of a species as the measure of its diversity. Ours should be enormous. Yet with what devotion we discourage the deviant in our midst, whether through the energies of despots, the calculations of the totalitarian state, or the sanctions of fashionable thought. How lustfully we destroy those who have most to give us— a Socrates, a Jesus Christ, a John Kennedy, a Martin Luther King. No gorilla, no musk ox could entertain a course so maladaptive, but only the human being. Yet we survive, while the mountain gorilla pursues a fading destiny in his shrinking, misty, bamboo forests and the musk ox makes his stand on a last few icy acres. It is a paradox within a paradox.

While we share many a trait with our animal kin, nothing about the human being can be regarded as commonplace. Could monkeys be puritans, they would condemn our sexuality as disgraceful. Could any in our primate family have been born an economist, he would regard us as mad, for we share our food, a practice almost without precedent. And beyond our primate family—in all the kingdom of vertebrate animals from fish to mice, excepting only a few dutiful birds —if thoughtful males existed, would they not look on our males with disapproval? We have humbly accepted the male role of provider for not only our young but also our females. At some moment or other in the human past, we may reflect, a feminine liberation movement must have scored an astonishing success.

We are different. The evolutionist's view of humankind suffers no distortion so gross as that "man is nothing but an animal." We can adapt to anything, whether storms at sea or the Arctic fringe or deserts that would discourage a lizard;

remarkably enough, we can adapt even to misery. Our skills are so obvious as to need no mention. Once we debated how many angels could dance on the head of a pin; now tens of thousands of electrons, at our command, dance on an area smaller. Yet we must beware of complacency. In all our skills, as in all our philosophies, something seems lacking, so much more skillful are we at implementing our antagonisms than our affections. How skillfully we lie, not only to each other but to ourselves. Most animals tell lies through camouflage, through mimicry, through false signals. I have detailed some examples in *The Social Contract* and need not pursue them here. But man, unique man, is the only animal who lies so skillfully as to deceive himself.

If man is a wonder, then what is wonderful must lie in the mass of his contradictions. The elephant in its own way, like the baboon, is a most logical animal, and could it know us better it would be most confused. Yet it knows us well enough to survive, as its extinct American cousins did not.

About twelve thousand years ago, at the end of the last great glaciation, skilled human hunters entered North America by way of the land bridge then exposed at the Bering Strait. Earlier wanderers may have come, but if they did they left small record. Now was a golden moment when the retreating ice sheet opened valley passages into America's interior, but the melting ice had not yet so lifted sea levels as to cover the land bridge. The new hunters, who would father the American Indian, left an unmistakable record: within a few thousand years they and their descendants, armed with only throwing spears and Asian sophistication, exterminated all the large game in both North and South America.

This thesis of "overkill," developed by Professor Paul Martin of the University of Arizona, reminds us that in our own last century we exterminated the modern bison, or American buffalo, in a spectacular demonstration of modern man's urge to kill and kill, without reference to economic

9

advantage. As mountaineers climb a mountain "because it's there," so we killed buffalo, even from passing trains. And so it is that every fossil record points to the probability that within a thousand years after our arrival in America across the land bridge we similarly exterminated the mammoth.

It was the mammoth of picture books, with hairy hide and deeply curved tusks. Since it was largely a grazer, it lived on the American western plains. Another cousin, the mastodon, was found most frequently in the eastern woodlands, where it could enjoy its favorite browse. There is no reason to suppose that either was less intelligent than the contemporary African elephant. But they were innocent. They knew nothing about man.

Despite the meditations of Jean-Jacques Rousseau there can be no initiation to catastrophe to compare with innocence. The African animals had evolved side by side with man, and the burden of our company had been such that they developed "flight distance" as the appropriate response when that small, dangerous animal appeared. It was natural selection of a classic order: those who developed the behavior pattern of flight distance when men appeared left more descendants than those who did not.

The mighty mammoth of North America died of innocence. It and the mastodon supported on their monumental legs about 25 percent of the continent's meat. As they must surely have been as intelligent as their African cousin, they must surely have been as formidable. But what good is might when you have never encountered the most dangerous of animals, the human being?

The hunting hypothesis may be stated like this:

Man is man, and not a chimpanzee, because for millions upon millions of evolving years we killed for a living.

Many a window looks out on the human scene, each with differing perspectives. For the past twenty years mine has been the window framed by contemporary evolutionary thought. I regard it then as legitimate to translate the question, Why is man man? into the question, Why are we not chimpanzees? I recognize that a century ago, in the day of Charles Darwin and Thomas Huxley, such a question would have been taken in a quite different way. These were the times when a lady of fashion is reputed to have cried, "We are descended from monkeys? Oh, I cannot believe it! But if it should be true, then pray God the word will not get around!" Well, the word did get around, so that while today our intimate relationship to the chimpanzee may be something that a few of us would rather not think about, it cannot be regarded as news. What must correctly concern us is not that we are like him, but that we are different.

No inquiry into the evolution of human uniqueness can ignore the hidden paradox that must lie somewhere near the heart of our nature. So it may be of value to state the hunting hypothesis in broader terms:

If among all the members of our primate family the human being is unique, even in our noblest aspirations, it is because we alone through untold millions of years were continuously dependent on killing to survive.

Fifteen years ago I could have made no statement so broad about the human being. We knew little enough at that time about human origins, and less about the chimpanzee. Even five years ago, when I published *The Social Contract*, while hints were sufficient to warrant speculation, hard evidence had not yet arrived from the field and the laboratory. Today, however, it is in hand.

In the sciences any hypothesis must be regarded as an informed guess seeking a central explanation for all the jigsaw bits of information available. As such it is subject to negation, modification, or confirmation as further information comes to light. Perhaps someday, when alternative explanations have been exhausted, it will have achieved the status of a theory. Such has been the history of the theory of evolution, but it will be seen that the life of a hypothesis is not a tranquil one.

In its simplest form the hunting hypothesis suggests that man evolved as a meat-eater. It is a new idea, offensive to many. Since the time of Darwin we had made the quite reasonable assumption that until we received that regal gift, the great brain, our ways had differed little from those of the inoffensive, vegetarian forest ape. Not till 1925 did anyone suggest otherwise. Then Professor Carveth Read of the University of London published his *Origins of Man*. He suggested that our earliest ancestors should be named *Lycopithecus*. He saw us, indeed, just as much wolflike as apelike, eating meat, hunting large game in packs. Since few read his book, no arguments broke out.

At about the same time, however, a South African professor of anatomy, Raymond A. Dart, was discovering Read's wolf-ape on the edge of the Kalahari Desert. The creature had a brain little larger than a chimpanzee but was otherwise quite human. Dart named him *Australopithecus*. Since the name is today familiar to every reader, I need mention here only that from the beginning Dart was convinced that the extinct creature was a member of our ancestral family, and from the evidence both of dentition and the barren environment which at no time could ever have supported forests and fruit, he was convinced likewise that the australopithecines were meat-eaters.

For decades his discovery remained inconspicuous, debated only by specialists. Then, in 1953, Dart published his paper *The Predatory Transition from Ape to Man*. By then the accumulation of South African evidence had convinced him that the australopithecines were not only meat-eaters but armed hunters. The title of his paper made the first direct statement of the hunting hypothesis, but no reputable scientific journal would print it. Largely unread, like Read's leap into speculation, it too started no arguments. Two years later I met Dart and inspected his evidence at the Johannesburg Medical School. I was not only convinced of its validity but convinced that what was being started represented a revolution in anthropology and in our estimates of man. On my return to the United States in the spring of 1955, I published my observations in New York's respected *Reporter* magazine. The following year I moved abroad to begin the five-year stint of research and writing that would add up to *African Genesis*.

These were Cold War years, dominated by our fears concerning the ultimate weapon. Like Dart, I was preoccupied by the implications of the hypothesis in terms of our ancient dependence on the weapon and on success in a violent life. I did not know, even when I was finishing the writing of my book in 1960, that a far broader statement of the implications had been delivered in 1956 at a Princeton symposium and later published. The statement was made by Professor S. L. Washburn, now at Berkeley, a man whom I believe to be the most creative of all American anthropologists. While at that date he was referring to the hunting experience of true large-brained man, still he made many a deduction that had not occurred to me. He wrote:

Hunting not only necessitated new activities and new kinds of cooperation but changed the role of the adult male in the group. Among the vegetarian primates, adult males do not share food. They take the best places for feeding and may even take food from less dominant animals. However, since sharing the kill is normal behavior for many carnivores, economic responsibility of the adult males and the practice of sharing food in the group probably resulted from being carnivorous. The very same actions that caused man to be feared by other animals led to food-sharing, more cooperation, and economic interdependence.

13

. . . The world view of the early human carnivore must have been very different from his vegetarian cousins. The desire for meat leads animals to know a wider range and to learn the habits of many animals. Human territorial habits and psychology are fundamentally different from those of apes and monkeys.

What Washburn's pioneer vision perceived was the *size* of the hunting hypothesis. Dart and I were concerned with the weapon fixation. But not just the pleasures of the chase or our exuberant partnership with the weapon had been fathered by our hunting past; we had also inherited those quite opposite qualities of cooperation, loyalty, responsibility, interdependence—a world view that the vegetarian primate could never know. And without these innovations man could never be man.

Surprisingly enough, despite Washburn's reputation, he elicited little from the sciences but the normal comments of "Very interesting." His thoughts were too far out. When *African Genesis* was published, the fat still avoided the fire, at least for a year or two. Although the book was widely read, I suspect that remote South African caves loaded with the remains of australopithecines and their half-million animal victims fell into the class of science fiction; besides, disreputable South Africa was an unsuitable site for the Creation. For quite other reasons of evidence I agreed. The South African fossil souvenirs, I recorded, seemed to me to commemorate the suburbs of human evolution. For the metropolis one must look two thousand miles to the north, to East Africa, and in particular to Kenya. My wife even contributed as one of her illustrations a drawing of that most remarkable of airport decorations, the signpost that shamelessly introduces you to Nairobi as the center of the human world. The signpost, as things turned out, was correct.

From about the time of *African Genesis* came discovery after discovery from the late Louis S. B. Leakey and his wife and son. I am convinced that they possess some mutant, radar-directed genes that discover human fossils as airport control towers discover approaching planes. Their discoveries mount to this day. The Leakeys not only have found the first man, but have found him three times.

Stormy days again whirled through African anthropology, which had always resembled not an institutionalized science but a form of guerrilla warfare. In the ripe South African days fossils had a mysterious way of disappearing, and reputations too. When Robert Broom at Sterkfontein discovered precisely the same australopithecine that Raymond Dart, many years earlier, had found at Taungs, he gave it the new name *Plesianthropus,* diminishing Dart's prior claim. When the scene shifted to East Africa, the tradition moved with it. Louis Leakey proclaimed the first of his famous discoveries as *Zinjanthropus,* although it was merely a variant of Broom's legitimate discovery *A. robustus,* a second and heavier-set species of australopithecine. Forced to retract, Leakey moved on to a later discovery, *Homo habilis,* and although it seemed to many simply an advanced form of Dart's *africanus,* he denied that it was an australopithecine at all. This was a bit too much even for Leakey's collaborators, John Napier and P. T. Tobias, who insisted that whether or not the being should be dubbed *Homo,* all these halfway beings were members or descendants of the australopithecine family.

Lest we lose our way in the semantic jungle, a warning must be posted. Dart's original definition of the australopithecines as beings with humanlike bodies, posture, and dentition, but brains closer in size to the ape than to man, furnished a radically new but rational bridge for the study of human evolution. According to that definition, no East African discovery much older than a million years can be regarded as any but specimens of the slow advance of the australopithecines to the status of true *Homo.* While the attempt by Louis Leakey—and the persistent efforts of his son, Richard—to establish the human line as quite unrelated to far northwestern Kenya, Richard Leakey near Lake Rudolf of Olduvai Gorge turned out to be 2 million years old. In the australopithecines most successfully crowds out Dart from the story of evolving man, it creates a disturbing image. It is as if the conquistadors in America denied Christopher Columbus. With worse philosophical implications, however, the Leakey insistence on man's unique origins raises once again the old specter of Special Creation. Bishop Wilberforce would be interested.

Despite transgressions that disturbed many a scientist, despite controversies that confused all but the most informed observer, it was the East African raid into our fossil past that fired the world's imagination. Radiogenic methods of absolute dating stunned all of anthropology. None had dared, in the time of *African Genesis,* to speculate on our ancestral antiquity much beyond a million years. Then the small-brained proto-men that the Leakeys were finding at the base and the American Clark Howell in the Omo Valley, all in the past few years, found a menagerie of hominid remains and artifacts going back almost 3 million years. With the Omo discoveries the search moved north to Ethiopia, where another American, Carl Johanson, together with a French group including Yves Coppens, had been working. In the autumn of 1974 the discovery of nine individuals was announced. They were very small, but straight-limbed and unquestionably of the hominid (man-tending, not ape-tending) line, with dates of well over 3 million years.

The Ethiopian discovery might seem the *ultima Thule* of anthropology's present probings. But it was not. A stroke of luck and justice directed that Mary Leakey, following her husband's death, should go back to a Tanzanian fossil bed in the Laetolil region not too far from the Olduvai Gorge, which they had explored together some forty years before. (Not all was luck, nor was all sentiment. Mary Leakey, as every African specialist knows, has been the most elegant sci-

16

entist in the family. But much was justice.) At Laetolil, in the summer of 1975, she found the remains of eleven individual hominids—eight adults, three children—whom she judges from dentition to have been meat-eaters. The date is certain. They are between 3.35 and 3.75 million years old.

Dr. Mary Leakey has topped the family's genius, but her discovery will not be the last. Dizzying though such human antiquity may seem, during Dr. Leakey's explorations Bryan Patterson had meanwhile found a single, undisputed hominid jaw west of Lake Rudolf at Lothagam Hill. Its date is a certain 5.5 million years.

Our South African estimates of 1961 had been picayune. Yet one of Dart's most startling claims, that a hominid with an ape-sized brain was capable of fashioning weapons and tools of bone, today remains beyond argument. From East Africa we have thousands of specialized, far more highly advanced stone implements, so meticulously analyzed by Mary Leakey. If Dart's southern gentlemen preferred the jawbones of antelope, we may attribute the preference simply to southern backwardness.

Among all the doubts and disagreements and semantic controversies that the rush of discovery has produced, what remains remarkable to this day is the resistance to the basic concept of our dependence on hunting. Even in the early 1960's two alternative hypotheses took root. One—a bit innocent and in fact a carry-over from earlier assumptions—we may call the vegetarian hypothesis. Meat was never important to evolving man, whose dependence was on plant foods. The other, favored by those authorities who knew the African background best, we may call the scavenger hypothesis. Until the brain of evolving man had expanded—say, half a million years ago—to sufficient degree, we were incapable of killing large prey. We lacked the capacities for cooperation, for tactics, for making and using adequate weapons. In our earlier, small-brained days we had hunted small game, slow

17

game, like fawns and tortoises. Any larger animals we had scavenged from the kills of such professional hunters as the lion and saber-tooth cat.

The scavenger hypothesis was so widely embraced by our most sophisticated authorities—Kenneth P. Oakley, Bernard Campbell, Louis Leakey himself—that it pervades our literature. Excellent logic granted its persuasions. We were small and not very fast, the physical counterpart of a modern ten-year-old boy. Our weapons, whether clubs or bones or shaped stones of no vast threat, were hand-held. How could we have killed any but the most vulnerable game? Anthropologists who knew the African sites at first hand could scarcely be infatuated with the vegetarian hypothesis, since there was the Makapan cave in South Africa with its half-million fossilized animal bones. There were the undoubted East African living sites in Olduvai Gorge Bed One—almost two million years old—with their kitchen middens of animal bones, many even smashed to extract the marrow. We ate meat. But we had not hunted.

I wondered from an early date about the popularity of the scavenger hypothesis. If we were incapable of killing large prey animals such as wildebeest and waterbuck, then how were we capable of stealing their remains from their rightful and more dangerous killers? If we had been concerned with only a few stray bones, then luck could account for it. But the impressive accumulations at early hominid living sites must indicate either that we had been even more adept thieves than we are today, or that the great carnivores in those times were unaccountably lazy at guarding their kills.

Some ingenious explanations were offered. Leakey himself suggested to many audiences that we had had nothing to fear from the great cats since we were not "cat food." Why? Because, since we too were meat-eaters, they did not like our flavor? It could be possible. Yet leopards specialize in killing village dogs, and competent observers have recorded leopards who find the jackal's taste so irresistible that they hunt little else. I find it difficult to believe that we tasted worse than jackals. Another ingenious explanation rests on the observed fact that men today, through loud threats, can drive even lions off a kill. But I have already mentioned the flight distance that is part of the survival equipment of almost every species when aware of human presence. That flight distance has been acquired through long, unhappy experience with man and such weapons as slaughtered the mammoth. I find my credulity strained at the picture of a cringing saber-tooth cat confronted by a few four-foot-tall hominids carrying clubs.

Washburn was another skeptic. In the early days of the scavenger hypothesis he dismissed it: hunting was easier. Man could have successfully scavenged only when he had become so dangerous, so well armed, that he could drive carnivores off their kill. Washburn was reversing the scavenger assumption: big-brained, big-bodied man might have had the skill to scavenge, but it was the small-brained, small-bodied hominid who would have had to hunt. Even so, no argument could be conclusive while we still lacked evidence.

So spectacular were the discoveries of early man that quite naturally the fascinations of the discoverers, of concerned scientists, and of the public at large focused on the human remains themselves. Analyzing the "faunal assemblage"—the thousands of associated animal bones, largely of extinct species, found at a living site—was a chore comparable to building a modest cathedral. First announcements therefore tended to be impressionistic. Leakey's assessment of fossil remains at the earliest Olduvai sites was that they consisted of very small or slow animals, which implied awkward, inexperienced hunters. The impression reinforced the scavenger hypothesis. By 1965, however, he was having second thoughts. In the first of the definitive volumes on Olduvai Gorge published by Cambridge University, he meditated on

19

the scarcity of fossil remains of very small antelopes, such as the duiker, the dik-dik, or the oribi. "This cannot be due to the bones of these species escaping notice, since thousands of bones of much smaller animals are in the collections. There must therefore be some other and at present unexplained reason for the scarcity of small antelope remains on the living floors of the early hominids."

By 1971 the scavenger hypothesis was gasping. Another Berkeley associate of Washburn's, Glynn Isaac, published an article called "The Diet of Early Man." Isaac, conservative by nature, with as long a personal experience as any in the East African field, denied in his paper the thesis that there had been no big-game hunting until the Middle Pleistocene and larger-brained *Homo erectus*. The faunal assemblages of early Olduvai reflected the same emphasis on larger antelopes and pigs that existed in the African fauna of the time. At one site so many examples of *Pelorovis*, a giant extinct goat about four times the size of a merino ram, had been found together that they seemed to indicate a drive in which the prey had been pressed into a morass. One even remains with his four fossilized legs standing vertical as if stuck in mud.

The same year the third volume of the Cambridge University Olduvai series appeared with Mary Leakey's detailed analysis of two definite slaughtering sites. These were not living sites where meat had been brought home from unknown sources, but the actual locations (quite probably like the presumed *Pelorovis* morass) where the animals had been trapped and butchered. One was an elephant as large as any present-day adult, the other a creature perhaps more formidable—the extinct *Dinetherium*. Over a hundred stone cutting-tools were mingled with the elephant remains. On a visit to Oxford in 1973 I consulted Dr. Kenneth P. Oakley, the now retired long-time head of the anthropology subdepartment of the British Museum (Natural History) and our foremost authority on fossil man. He has permitted me to publish his statement:

> The fossil presence of very large prey animals, such as elephant and the extinct *Dinetherium*, at butchering sites in the Olduvai Gorge almost two million years old —long before any evidence for the modern human brain— amounts to proof that hunting had been practiced systematically and successfully for unknown earlier periods of time by the evolving, small-brained ancestral hominid.

Since I was in the United States the following winter, I called Professor Washburn in Berkeley and told him that I intended to use his 1956 quotation concerning the relation of hunting to our nature, but that I didn't want to be guilty of using it out of context. He had been describing it in terms of true larger-brained *Homo;* could I use it in the context of our earlier, small-brained past? "Of course," he said. "We know we've been hunting for three million years, and God knows how much longer than that."

The new view was being reinforced by other than physical anthropologists assessing the implications of recent fossil discoveries. By 1970 there were beginning to appear the first of the major studies of the great carnivores who would have been our competitors in ancient predatory communities. *Innocent Killers,* by two of our most famous students of animals in a state of nature, Jane Goodall and Hugo van Lawick, expressed clearly a common conclusion. After Goodall's long work with chimpanzees, she shifted her attentions to predators, partly out of curiosity concerning the ways of early man. She had been impressed that her chimpanzees, though they enjoyed meat and frequently hunted, never scavenged. Furthermore, she had never seen baboons join a scavenging group, although they have a taste for meat. True predators, on the other hand, will scavenge any time they can get away with it. Goodall concluded that evolving man, a perfect opportunist, would have scavenged too when he could get away with it. But his opportunities would always have been rare. We were too badly equipped for the competition.

We lack the natural predators' keenness of smell and hearing. High in the sky the vulture, with its superb eyesight, can be the first to spot a dying animal or a kill, and with a swoop of wings it can be the first to arrive. His movement will be the signal to all of us, including hyenas and even lions, that a meal is being served. But we can't get there fast enough—the hyena can do thirty miles an hour—and getting there first is important. Goodall's sophistication does not permit her to see a band of small, early, ill-armed proto-men driving a clan of hyenas or a pride of lions off a kill. Once in a lucky while it might have happened, but we could not have had survived on it.

So long as we were dependent on meat for survival, we were dependent on hunting. The scavenging hypothesis is ended. But the other alternative, the vegetarian hypothesis, is another matter. Just how much we could have depended on plant foods, I leave until a later chapter.

Not quite ten thousand years ago we initiated that overwhelming cultural invention, the domestication of cereals and legumes—wheat, barley, beans—and the domestication of such animals as goats and sheep and cattle. The invention spread slowly. Until five thousand years ago it affected the fate, the life expectancy, the conditions of freedom or servitude of a very small fraction of the human population. It is not the end of the human story, since from a dramatist's point of view it is the beginning of the third act, the world we know. We gained control over nature—or at least, so we assumed—whereas earlier we had been portions of nature, as much its actors as the sensitive impala, the lurking cheetah, the defiant elephant cow, the surprising crocodile. We were one species—increasingly dangerous—among others.

It takes arithmetic's small beer to compare such a 5,000 years with the time of our beginnings. To a degree—but to a degree only—it matters little whether we accept for early days the scavenger or the hunting hypothesis. In any case, we accept the notion that hunting dominated our lives for a good 500,000 years, leaving an eye-blink of 5,000 for our present state. For a mere one percent of the history of true man, we have lived under conditions which we regard as normal.

Yet can any reader regard the 99 percent of human history during which we were dependent on hunting as insignificant? I speak of perhaps 25,000 generations. Throughout that time natural selection accepted or discarded individuals or groups hunters. Are we to believe, as so many victims of fashionable thought will assert, that such selection left no mark on us? Why then, if rationality is all, should anyone reject our history as hunters? This is why I wondered at the popularity of the scavenger idea. Yet I begin to understand. It blocks a further inquiry into the origins of the human brain.

Half a million years ago is plenty, in terms of modern genetics, to explain certain human propensities for the chase and the kill, for cooperation, for the male role of provider. If you failed to do these things through 25,000 generations then with little doubt, according to Darwinian differential in terms of a single standard, our capacity to survive as reproduction, you left fewer descendants than the next man. But there was a catch, a door left open. All this happened only *after* the enlargement of the human brain. We acted by rational choice, not by animal compulsion (an overrated factor, but let it go). If we chased and killed, if we sacrificed ourselves in the effort, if we shared our meat, if we listened to our leader, then we were acting like human beings *because* we were human beings. Our brain had stepped in to make decisions of calculation and self-interest.

But what if the hunting way, with all the human consequences that Washburn implied, had started millions of years *before* the advent of the human brain? Then our brain—like our triceps, our buttocks, our flattened running feet—is an evolutionary consequence of survival necessities that had come before.

I must dwell on this, since it is not only the premise for this inquiry into the evolution of human uniqueness, but an intellectual Rubicon across which few have ventured. *Are the qualities that we regard as uniquely human the consequence of being human beings, or have we evolved as human beings because of the earlier evolution of qualities that we regard as uniquely human?*

It is the central question. Are we to continue to accept, as we have accepted for so long, that the advent of the great human brain meant the advent of all things human? That it came to us like the coughed-up gift of an immaculate fish? That with its incredible multiplication of neurons it made all things possible, including humanity? That it is a magnificent implement without history, without memories? I cannot accept it.

Our brain, like our straight backs and our running feet, came about as one more adventure in the long human story—and the mightiest. It came about through natural selection as a complex of organs, some old, some new, of profound survival value to an evolving line of beings. It came as an answer to necessities that for millions of years had been growing more complex. It presented us with a few new problems, too, that remain unsolved. But all in all it brought us a means of doing better what we had already been doing anyway.

This is a story about our evolutionary past, and how it remains part of us. While it may explain why we are human beings and not chimpanzees, the story will not explain how we are to remain human beings. Our humanity evolved as a portion of our hunting way, and the hunting way, regrettably, is gone.

24

Paradise Lost

For tens of millions of years benevolence had enfolded the earth. The Antarctic ice cap, if it existed at all, was no more than a frosty patch. With none or little of the earth's waters locked in upland ice sheets and glaciers, sea levels were high, the seas warm. Where today stand most of the world's great cities, then stood the seas' margins, several hundred feet deep.

It was a remarkable world. Rains were reliable. A broad equatorial forest reached from westernmost Africa to the ends of Asia. No stark Arabian desert broke the green continuity. Tree-savannah Arabia may have been, or lightly wooded prairies; but forest gentry in East Africa could still exchange genetic greetings with their Indian fellows, as the fossil record shows. Not even the Red Sea offered an impediment to travel, since it seems to have consisted of a series of briny lakes. Only three or four million years ago, with the twisting of continents, did the Straits of Bab-el-Mandeb open to bar the Afro-Asian wanderings of our early primate family.

The Miocene world of twenty million years ago little resembled our own. Not even the sky at night was the same. Constellations familiar to us had not all reached their present configurations, and while many of their stars have died, many of ours had not been born. Yet perhaps the most conspicuous of all changes was the lack in those times of certain qualities that we take for granted: glory, ambition, self-delusion, hope, despair. There were no people then.

The Miocene was the time of the ape. The earth had basked

in the benevolence of warmth and rains and forest affluence for so many tens of millions of years that sufficient time had elapsed for our entire primate family to evolve. We were forest specialists. There is firm speculation that when the mammals took over a world surrendered by the reptiles, rodents inherited the ground as we inherited the trees. In the beginning we were all nocturnal, as most rodents remain. A few living fossils of early primate times—the bush-baby, for example, or Madagascar's mouse lemur—still exhibit the great, round, moist nocturnal eyes seemingly copied from those saccharine paintings of children so popular in Paris. Almost all of us, however, as monkeys came along, and then apes, became daytime beings.

Our diurnal way was to become critically important to evolving man at a far later date. Back in the Miocene and even earlier times, the selective advantage of daytime vision presumably lay in our way of life. Leaping or swinging from bough to bough, we bettered our chances of survival if we could see what we were doing. The same survival pressure encouraged stereoscopic vision, depth perception, the loss of rodentlike claws, and their replacement by flattened nails protecting sensitive finger-pads. We may watch with awe the acrobatics of the high-flying gibbon, yet even for him his heights present hazard; a fair number of wild gibbons carry the scars of broken bones. You need all the helpful adaptations you can manage to survive in the trees.

While the loss of claws denied us a traditional weapon, it provided a significant inheritance: the flexible, grasping hand. Perhaps it was this exploring, manipulating, ever investigating primate hand that supported from tarsier to ape a continually increasing dependence on learning and memory, a decreasing dependence on stereotyped instinct. Our reasoning power, however, is scarcely unique to man; it is simply the peak of a trend that we share with all lemurs, all monkeys, all apes.

26

Unlike the ape of today—rare, shy, trapped in a few remnants of ancient forest—the ape of the Miocene was a common animal. He was common everywhere from Europe to Africa to Asia. But he never reached the New World, which long before had drifted away from the Old, and that is why no trace of evolving man can be found in the Americas. Our interest in Miocene East Africa rests solely on hindsight, on our present knowledge that here was where man departed from the old ape stock and went his own evolutionary way. So we rummage among the species of the time. Most undoubtedly fathered nothing but extinction, although a giant, *Proconsul major,* may have been ancestral to the modern gorilla. What must interest us is the chimpanzee. At some moment in the ancient forest there was an ape ancestral to us both.

Various workers in the fields of immunology and molecular genetics have demonstrated the closeness of our relationship to the chimp, as in an example familiar to readers of Jane Goodall. In the course of her long study of wild chimpanzees near Lake Tanganyika, polio broke out in an African village. The disease spread rapidly to members of the group she was studying, crippling and killing them in precisely the same fashion in which it attacks human beings. Although she could not know that our oral vaccine would work with chimps, in the emergency she had a supply flown out from Nairobi. To those yet unaffected, she administered the vaccine hidden in bananas. The epidemic was immediately checked.

One investigator, Berkeley's Vincent Sarich, created a momentary sensation in the sciences with his conclusion that the "immunological distance" between chimp and man is so little that our evolutionary ways must have parted no more than 5 or 6 million years ago. The conclusion was satisfactory to neither biologists nor paleontologists. The fossil jaw from Lothagam Hill, which I have described as over 5 million years old, shows no significant ape affinities. Sarich's date was far too recent. Nevertheless, such studies have demonstrated the closeness of our relationship, and have sharpened the question, Why are we human beings and not chimps?

I myself go along with the widespread assumption that we must look to the Miocene forest for the still undiscovered ape who carried both the human and the chimp potential. Only in such a setting of forest abundance could the chimp have retained his dietary dependence on fruit. It has been the tragedy of the ape that, having evolved in an environment of affluence, he could not survive without it.

Several odd and quite disparate lines of evidence and speculation tie together when we try to draw mental pictures of our common ancestor. The first was the brain child of the neglected Dutch ethologist Adriaan Kortlandt, who offered the startling notion that such a common ancestor may have had a closer resemblance to man than to the chimp. Indeed, it was something more than a notion, if less than a hypothesis. Kortlandt had studied wild forest chimpanzees in the eastern Congo, captive chimps at the zoo in Amsterdam, the records of comparable captives from a wide range of zoos around the world, and a group living in a semiwild setting at Conakry, Guinea. He had come to a radical conclusion: natural selection in a normal environment could not account for chimpanzee capacities in an experimental setting.

There was the matter of weapons, for example. Through the studies of Jane Goodall, we know far more today about the chimp in the wild than did Kortlandt over a decade ago. We know that a chimp will on occasion seize a stick and brandish it like a weapon at an opponent. Yet the stick seems more an instrument of display than of violence. Not infrequently a chimp will throw a stone—or he may try to hurl as unsuitable a missile as a bunch of leaves. The chimp in the wild does not seem to have the "idea" of the weapon. But in captivity, he has.

One reliable record was that of a zoo-born chimp who had never seen a leopard, let alone a weapon. When he was taken for his first walk by the keeper, he approached a leopard cage, sighted its occupant, fell over backward in terror, and fled. The keeper calmed him. But before the youngster would continue his walk he secured a stick, and gripped it tightly. He then consented to walk past the leopard cage. The most important part of the record is a footnote: he would never again take a walk in that direction without arming himself first.

There is scarcely a zoo without some such record, as there is scarcely a zoo without a long history of chimps' hurling objects at visitors. That they will urinate on you with excellent aim, I can myself bear witness. That they will go to lengths both more creative and objectionable, was once the subject of a diplomatic incident at the London Zoo. The visitor was the head of an African state who habitually appeared in full dress uniform. Warned of his approach, the keepers panicked. I don't know whether their prize chimpanzee was a racist or whether he simply disliked medals, but they cleaned his cage of carrots and all other loose objects. When the visitor appeared to admire him, the chimp took one look, made a round of his cage, found nothing throwable, and quickly squeezed out some feces and let go with unpardonable accuracy. It took all the apologies of the Foreign Ministry to convince the visitor that the chimp had not been trained to do it.

Kortlandt once showed me film of an experiment he had made at the Amsterdam Zoo. A chimp who had never seen a tiger (in the wild it would be impossible, since they come from different continents) was placed in a cage liberally scattered with brick-sized wooden blocks. The tiger was introduced to the next cage. The chimp's response was instant. He bounced block after block off the wire barrier separating the cages.

Even more impressive was film that Kortlandt had made in Conakry. Here a fair group of chimpanzees were kept in a large quarry with walls high enough to prevent escape. Kort-landt scattered about a few straight sticks, whose lengths varied to that of clothes poles. Then, at the top of the wall where visitors usually came to watch, he exhibited a tame leopard. At the sight of their natural enemy the chimpanzees rose, significantly, to bipedal posture. Also significantly, they did not flee but charged. And as they charged they picked up the poles on their way, hurling them like spears against the wall. Their aim was poor, their charge futile, but the armed attack told much about a chimpanzee potential that is difficult to explain.

Not in the forest and not on its savannah margins have we ever observed such behavior in wild chimpanzees. How did it enter into the unlearned repertory of chimpanzee behavior? Kortlandt's answer would be that in the forest the chimpan-zee has degenerated, but that our common ancestor behaved more like men. It is a wild answer, but two very recent obser-vations have reminded me of it.

Several widely publicized experiments have left no doubt that the chimp can be taught a language. Many years ago the hope was abandoned when two very competent psycholo-gists in Florida, raising a young chimp as they would their own child, failed to teach her more than four spoken words. Then, beginning in 1966, Allen and Beatrice Gardner at the University of Nevada took a different approach. If the chimp brain lacked the speech center that has developed in ours, it evidently did not lack a center controlling the manipulation of fingers and hands. So they adopted a young female named Washoe and gradually introduced her to the deaf-and-dumb language known in the United States as Amslan, in which each gesture represents a word or concept.

Two years later David Premack, in Santa Barbara, launched a comparable experiment with another young female named Sarah. But instead of sign language, Sarah was introduced to plastic chips with a thin magnetized backing that could stick to a metal plate. The chips varied in arbitrary symbols and colors which could be arranged to form messages, even sentences. The success of both experiments has been too stunning and too recent to be absorbed as yet by students of chimpanzees or men. It was not just that the chimp could learn a large vocabulary (in Washoe's case about 160, in Sarah's at my last report, 130), or that they could quite easily grasp such concepts as *you, they, me,* but that syntax came almost as easily as to a human child. You did not signal *me give* if what you meant was *give me.* A thoughtful study of these experiments and others has been made in Eugene Linden's very recent *Apes, Men and Language.*

The pioneer ethologist Professor W. H. Thorpe of Cambridge has been fascinated by the chimpanzee experiments and their implications concerning a fundamental but assumed distinction between animals and men. He writes:

> It would no doubt be easy to devise definitions of language such that no examples of animal communications could readily find inclusion therein. There have always been, and no doubt there will continue to be, those who resist with great vigor any conclusions which seem to break down what they regard as one of the most important lines of demarcation between animals and men. We must surely be justified in accepting such preconceived definitions only with the utmost caution.

As Thorpe implies, the blurring of the distinctions between men and other animals which the last few decades of research have brought about has inflicted dismay on many a traditionalist. But the achievements of Sarah and Washoe and more chimps now being studied have brought evolutionary problems too. How could such a capacity have evolved in a state of nature? On a grander scale, it is the case of Kortlandt's weapons. And another puzzler has surfaced.

Jane Goodall's ten-year study of wild chimpanzees is best

read in her magnificent volume *In the Shadow of Man,* published in 1971. In short early papers she had administered a series of shocks to what we thought we knew about chimpanzees. Their capacity to make a purposeful tool rocked a few anthropological boats. That they periodically, systematically hunt and kill smaller animals rocked my own boat. Goodall estimated that about twenty times a year members of her band went hunting. A later specialized study by the Hungarian-American Geza Teleki raises the estimate to about thirty forays. To add to the confusion, we now have two authentic observations of cannibalism in which adult males have killed and eaten young chimps. Nor can we ascribe this gruesome development to such charitable interpretations as hunger, deprivation, or somebody's sulks. One of the villains, as described by J. D. Bygott, was the alpha male Humphrey, a solid citizen observed throughout the length of Goodall's study.

Leaving aside cannibalism, chimpanzee hunting raises a single question: why? Some cases seem spontaneous, like the impulsive smashing of a young baboon. Others are as purposeful and cooperative as the actions of a lion pride. In no cases may the event be described as nutritional. If evolving man hunted for a living, the chimpanzee hunts for fun. A ten-pound monkey contributes few calories to the shared diet of half a dozen adult chimps. And shared it is, for this is the one situation in which primates share food.

Teleki looks on hunting as a recently acquired characteristic, a conclusion with which few authorities, I believe, would agree. The social consequences of a kill are entirely too formalized and too contrary to normal chimpanzee behavior, involving too many inhibitions. Rules and regulations govern the social procedure. The kill, without argument, is the sole possession of the one who achieved it. He may be subadult without social rank. He eats in peace, surrounded by his superiors waiting hopefully for a hand-out. Graciously he dispenses a bit here, a bit there among the outstretched palms. In one observed case a high alpha waited for hours and received nothing. Accepted possession by the killer, remarkably enough, is precisely the same as the behavior of wolves described by David Mech.

So I return to the question, Why do they hunt? No other ape does. In George Schaller's study of the mountain gorilla he examined thousands of scats without finding a bone or a scrap of fur. Only that oversized monkey, the savannah baboon, hunts and kills, but his is a seasonal occupation when gazelle fawns are dropped. It may also be a regional activity, since Irven DeVore and Washburn never witnessed it in over a thousand hours of baboon observation. Among chimpanzees, hunting is an institution almost exclusively male, unrelated to need for food. Meat is not the object; significantly, they will not touch carrion, even freshly killed, nor are they interested in the kills of any but their local social group.

One cannot ignore an evolutionary question simply because one has no answer for it, so I return to Kortlandt's wild guess. Is it possible that our common ancestor was more manlike than chimplike? That he hunted? That in the hunting life he used weapons in defense and attack? That he came to enjoy meat, if not to depend on it for survival, and to enjoy the hunt? That in the hunting life he developed an intellectual potential that the chimp was not to need in his later forest life? In other words, are the capacities of the chimpanzee which natural selection cannot explain in terms of a forest environment indeed souvenirs of the time of our common ancestors?

There is one more possible piece for the puzzle. Since 1961 a scruffy problem has hung about the back door of anthropology, offering so little in the way of solution that many authorities have wished it would just go away. I described it in another context in *The Social Contract,* so I shall be brief about it here. In 1960, in western Kenya, Louis Leakey discovered the Fort Ternan site, a limited area in which an enormous quantity of animal bones lay scattered about. He showed me photographs that year with the simple comment "You never saw so many bones." They were superbly fossilized by an ashfall. (East Africa's history has been that of one volcanic outburst after another, which—while providing unpleasantness for those caught out lacking asbestos umbrellas —has been the delight of the paleontologist, so perfectly are fossils preserved. And the ash can be dated.) The Fort Ternan bones were so numerous that Leakey found a thousand in the first season of digging.

The following season he found what he named *Kenyapithecus* and claimed to be a hominid, of the human, not the ape, line. The date was secure if astounding—14 million years old—but it was not much of a fossil, just a fair fragment of an upper jaw. Elwyn Simons of Yale became curious. Back in the 1930's much work had been done on a variety of Miocene apes found in India's Siwalik Hills. G. E. Lewis, also of Yale, had found one which he believed to be hominid and named *Ramapithecus*. Simons did his digging in the Yale collection and found that it almost perfectly matched Leakey's discovery—with the same curved, arched palate and small canine teeth—and that it was more or less contemporary with Leakey's. They were either of the same species or closely related, so according to scientific custom the earlier discovery took priority. The name *Ramapithecus* replaced *Kenyapithecus* in publications written by others than Louis Leakey. But both fragments were of the upper jaw. Simons, dissatisfied, continued his rummaging through museum collections for fossils overlooked or wrongly classified. He found the lower jaw of still another Indian specimen fitted perfectly the ramapithecine fragments.

There remained little doubt that the family was of our stock. In his *Early Man* Clark Howell wrote, "One simply does not find a jaw like *Ramapithecus*' on the body of a quadrupedal animal any more than one would find grasping toes associated with the fossil remains of a horse." Nevertheless, many problems remained. We know that the Indian branch of the family became extinct, along with the true Indian apes. If the Kenya branch is ancestral to man, then it is almost ten million years older than any hominid fossil so far discovered. What happened to us in the meantime?

To complicate things further, in a later season of expanding excavation the Leakeys made another discovery at Fort Ternan. They found a small area where the animal bones— mostly antelope, just as at Olduvai—had been smashed by some implement to extract the marrow. No hyena could have done the job. I have never visited the site, but late in 1971, less than a year before he died, Louis and I spent a few days together in California. At that time he showed me his photographs of animal remains fossilized so rapidly by the ashfall that antelope leg-bones remained jointed; photographs of bones dented and smashed; and photographs of a worn lump of lava which he regarded as the implement. If he was correct, then it is our first known tool.

Were the ramapithecines close to the common ancestor of chimp and man? Is it possible that even in that time of abundance our line had embarked on the hunting, meat-eating, tool-using way? Or was it an early experiment that failed, to occur again much later when times were less fruitful, meat more necessary?

I do not know. If I revive the question in the context of the chimpanzee riddle, it is not because I am ready with an answer. Rather, it is to point to the complexity of questions. The evolutionist himself may fall into the fallacy of the laboratory psychologist with his simplified rat whose only motive is gaining a food pellet; in the same way, we with our concern for the past and the forces of natural selection may find ourselves chained to the economic determinism of Karl Marx or Adam Smith. We are then helpless to explain why a

35

chimp should take pleasure in hunting when he does not need meat, or why some vaguely known Miocene being in the midst of affluence found similar delights. Motivation, chimp or human, may look to horizons beyond today's hamburgers or tomorrow's potatoes. We may even note that certain young people in our time, to the bewilderment of their elders, found only boredom in an affluent society.

The marks of the past may lie long upon us.

Just before World War II, the British ornithologist David Lack went out to the Galapagos Islands to study Darwin's finches. There in 1835 Charles Darwin, in the course of the voyage of the Beagle, came on the remarkable variety of species of these drab little birds, each adapted to one way of life or another. He recognized that the finches could have arrived on the remote islands only through some ancient accident—blown in a storm, perhaps—and that by no stretch of the statistical imagination could fourteen different species have been caught up by the same accident. Besides, there was not one that resembled a living species on the South American mainland. A now-extinct species had arrived on the Islands; through slow adaptation, slow subdivision it had evolved into the varied birdlife he found around him.

In that thundering hour on those lonely, monotonous coasts and uplands, Charles Darwin was confronted with the evidence for natural selection. Not for several more years did he grasp the whole principle. And it would be almost a quarter of a century until he published his book.

So Darwin's inconspicuous finches took their place in the history of human thought, and so Lack returned to make a definitive study of their various adaptations. Few other birds had ever reached the Islands, so they faced few competitors. No woodpeckers, for example, had ever arrived, so a woodpecking niche was open. And one famous species of finch, poorly equipped by nature for such a trade, took to using a tool—a spine of cactus—for fishing out larvae from beneath bark. Others developed stout beaks, suitable for cracking hard seed; still others, slim curved beaks for probing flowers for nectar. For most creatures the Galapagos Islands rate low on nature's listing of attractive real estate, but for finches they were heaven.

High among finch attractions was a total lack of predators. Two small species of owl and hawk were there, but they seem to have offered no problems. Of falcons, large hawks, and the like, there were none. Since whatever date the ancestral species of finch had been blown from the mainland, no Galapagos finch had ever seen a dangerous hawk. How long had that been? When one considers that the original species as well as its mainland relative are extinct, and that fourteen descendant species have evolved since, one must reckon conservatively in terms of hundreds of thousands of years, possibly a million.

The point of the story, as so often happens, exists as a footnote that is not even a part of Lack's book. When he left the Islands he brought away quite a few caged finches for further study in England. About the time he reached the Panama Canal, war was declared, and Lack recognized that this was an awkward moment to be arriving at Oxford with a load of birds. He sent them on to a colleague, Robert Orr, in Marin County, California. Thirty specimens arrived, drawn from four species. To Orr's disbelief, every bird reacted with alarm to the sight of a red-tailed hawk, a turkey vulture, a raven—any predator bird. When from his office he heard an alarm call from an aviary, he knew that a hawk was in sight. Even fledglings would crouch. A possible million years had been insufficient to erase an ancient experience of terror.

In his recent book *Chance and Necessity*, the French molecular biologist and Nobel laureate Jacques Monod writes:

> Everything comes from experience; yet not from actual experience, reiterated by each individual with each

37

generation, but instead from experience accumulated by the entire ancestry of the species in the course of its evolution.

The evolutionary experience of man can hardly be compared to the evolutionary experience of Galapagos finches. I have described as a characteristic of our primate evolution the gradual freeing from our dependence on stereotyped instinct, and, aided by the enlarging brain, our growing dependence on individual learning. But this does not mean that we are the *tabula rasa* of behaviorist assumption. Even John Watson, the no-compromise founder of the behaviorist movement, conceded at least one human instinct: the infant's fear of falling. The value of such an instinct would have been meaningless through the millions of years that we have lived on the ground. It must go back to a time when, like baboons, we still slept in trees; it may go back to the Miocene forest itself.

Difficult though it may be to penetrate the mysteries of times so long ago, still nothing lacks relevance to the way we are. It may be unimportant to solve the riddle of chimpanzee and man. Still, there is value in learning that our closest relative has his paradoxes too. Immense though the speculative bridge must be that carries us on to a time of firm evidence, still the bridge does not cross unknown chasms. For there were problems in Paradise.

Even by the time of the ramapithecines, the weather was deteriorating. Imperceptibly the world was beginning to cool. Perhaps the change came in waves a million years long, then in shorter cycles. Or perhaps, more simply, there were those seasons when the rains failed to come—rare at first, more frequent later. It meant that the endless forests which had sheltered us, nourished us, provided our security, presented us with the original womb wherein the primate family was born, were thinning, shrinking.

The good times were over. Yet just possibly it was a freak-ishness of East African geology that prepared Kenya as the human cradle. Those who are familiar with mile-high Nairobi and central Kenya's high, sweeping savannahs, bisected north and south by the quarter-mile-deep Rift Valley, are not look-ing at the landscape that prevailed five or ten million years ago. A geological survey published in 1971 must quite change our view. Except for the looming volcanoes, much of Kenya was then a tropical lowland. What we see today is a broad dome some six hundred miles wide, most of which has been uplifted in the past three million years. Yet many a pocket may have earlier hung on, many a flourishing river course, not a few swamps for crocodile pleasure in the ancient Kenya lowland.

In general, the time of the ape was over. He was a fair-weather animal. This was the time when in India the numer-ous species, including the related ramapithecines, became extinct. One survivor, the nine-foot-tall *Gigantopithecus*, making his peace for a while with the spreading grassland, somehow found a living eating seeds but vanished in the later Pleistocene. Perhaps he gave up finally out of sheer boredom. A few—the orang, the gibbon, and the related siamang—were pressed into smaller and smaller tropical areas of Southeast Asia. The gorilla and chimp moved westward in Africa with the remaining forests. (Whatever the chimp's enthusiasm for hunting, he was unable to survive on it.) Fruit, shoots, buds, a few leaves, insects, and bird's eggs were the ape's staff of life. With the coming of the Pliocene, the pantry simply vanished.

Something different, however, happened in Kenya, and the difference would some day be man. In *African Genesis* I rashly put forward what is known as the deprivation hy-pothesis. Smaller, weaker, more poorly adapted to life in the trees than the great forest apes, we could not compete, and so we took to the spreading savannahs, the thriving herds of

39

grazing animals, and the meat-eater's way. The hypothesis was well received, particularly by those who were far from the evidence. For excellent reason it was less well received by sophisticated critics. On the savannah we would have died. (As is my shameless custom, I have long since—and publicly—retracted the hypothesis, having learned from my betters.)

The problem is one of preadaptation. Had not certain minimum qualifications evolved before our journey to the open-air butcher shop, our chances for survival would have been hopeless. An example of preadaptation is the nesting habit of the American chimney swift. The immediate question arises, What was the chimney swift doing before he had chimneys to nest in? Well, he nested in hollow trees, and there were not many chimney swifts. This is preadaptation. When chimneys came along, the species had a population explosion.

Human preadaptation involved three qualities without which there could never have been human beings: bipedal locomotion, freed hands, and weapons. Our bipedal posture might be awkward and our feet poorly adapted, but if we had to keep dropping to all fours like the knuckle-walking ape, then our hands were not free. And if our hands were not free, and flexible enough to grasp the crudest weapon with minimum skill, then we were not in business.

The three basic assets may be regarded as a syndrome. All are tied neatly together, and it does not matter particularly which evolved first. Yet I must assert a basic tenet of Darwinian evolution: things do not evolve with purpose. We cannot, for today's survival necessities, develop answers for an unknown tomorrow. We could not, even in millions of years, evolve assets for the purpose of going hunting some day. If we forget the familiar portrait of Kenya, however—the high savannah such as we see today—and think of it as considerably occupied by tropical lowlands with lingering stands of dense forest, then ecologically things begin to make sense.

Our forest-ape ancestors of the Miocene were probably

small. It is true that the leg-bones of Richard Leakey's remarkable discoveries from East Lake Rudolf indicate a stature of five feet four, with an indicated age of 2.6 million years, but there is nothing like them until we come down to modern man. The hundreds upon hundreds of examples of small-brained man from East and South Africa indicate a stature of about four feet. Johanson's discoveries in Ethiopia, made too recently for definitive dating or analysis but probably a million years older than Richard Leakey's, come closer to expectation. Leg-bones there indicate a stature of about three feet six.

This matter of size has importance. A band of heavy modern chimpanzees or gorillas, existing on low-calorie fruits, buds, and shoots, requires many square miles of forage. A family of lightweight gibbons in Thailand—highly territorial —can exist nicely on a private property of two hundred acres. The lingering forest stands in Kenya could have supported adequately, if not luxuriously, not the great apes but our smaller ancestors. Quite possibly it was the time of final separation between the emigrating great apes and our less-demanding ancestors.

I must emphasize that all I write about this transitional period is speculative, since we have no fossil evidence. But there is another factor of size. The heavy apes proceeding on all fours support their fore-weight on the backs of their hands—the position known as knuckle-walking. That is why you find no hair on the backs of a gorilla's fingers. But the lightweight gibbon can proceed for quite a distance on two legs, balancing himself like a tightrope walker who has had one too many.

I favor a supposition that a taste for meat, a hunting disposition, and perhaps even the use of weapons, were dispositions of our common Miocene ancestor. But chimp dentition indicates no departure from the fruit-eating way, while ours does, even in the faraway times of the ramapithecines. The chimp

41

retained his love for meat, which even today affects his social arrangements, but he was never dependent on it for survival. We became so. Even presuming that our diet remained largely fruit, in post-Miocene Kenya the forested islands of our former Eden became more and more widely separated by grasslands.

In 1953—the same year that Dart published his *Predatory Transition from Ape to Man*—two eminent American ecologists, George Bartholomew and J. M. Birdsell, published a paper that cannot be ignored by any student of human evolution. It was called *Ecology and the Protohominids,* and unlike Dart's it was published in that dowager of scientific journals, *American Anthropologist.* The authors made two eternal points: First, there is nothing sacred about traveling on two feet, since any four-footed animal can outrun us, so its selective value must have rested on the freeing of the hands. Second, no vulnerable primate could have survived on the African savannah had he not carried a weapon in his hand. (We were without claws. Kortlandt has described us as wolves carrying our fangs, like dentures, in our hands.)

In a Kenya environment such as I have described, it became necessary for us to cross open spaces. These open spaces were attracting prey animals and their camp-followers, the predators. Among prey species there was the hipparion, for example, a three-toed horse, now extinct, that entered Europe from America twelve million years ago. In forest days he browsed on leaves and buds. But perhaps his long history of migration had equipped him to deal with anything, so that as the grasslands spread he became a grazer. In the time I describe, he existed in luscious herds. How could the predator tell us, in terms of protein, from the hipparion? Meat is meat.

We were as much at the mercy of the predator as any other savannah creature. Fruit-dependent chimps must move many miles to find an area where fruit is ripening. Their size and their power discourage the predator, and in the continuous forest there are always trees for refuge. We had no such size, no such power, nor—in the broken landscape of the old Kenya lowlands—could we count on the all-saving trees. Crossing predator-hunted meadows between fruit-bearing forest clumps would have been a high-risk venture without some kind of expedient weapon in our hand. And so, for defensive purposes, preadaptation for hunting and meat-eating came about.

To carry a weapon demanded free hands. To free our hands, a degree of erect posture and bipedal movement, however awkward, became a necessity. And so every selective pressure favored those of us who most reliably could stand erect and move on two feet, just as it favored those newly freed hands that could most ably wield a weapon. Perhaps as our capacities increased we used our weapons not entirely to defend ourselves, but on occasion to knock down a small, slow animal and so supplement our diet of fruit with odd bits of meat. Whether we did or we didn't, we were being preadapted for the hunting life, though millions of years might pass before the final reduction of forest made meat-eating a survival necessity.

In this time of transition a notable biological change was overtaking the prehuman being. We became cultural animals. It is a phrase I am lifting from Professor Robin Fox of Rutgers, although I believe I am using it in a somewhat different way. My stress lies on a biological consequence of a cultural acquisition. Throughout this narrative I shall frequently refer to *irreversibility*. We invent or adopt a cultural asset to aid our survival but, through a process of feedback, we lose the natural asset to deal with the same situation. Thus we become continuously dependent on the cultural acquisition for survival. And we cannot go back. So it was with the cultural acquisition of the weapon in the hand, whether an expedient

43

club of wood or bone or stone. The cultural acquisition made redundant our fighting teeth.

Just as we are the only primate who in our evolutionary past became dependent on meat for survival, so we are the only primate to suffer reduction of the long, sharp canine teeth characteristic of our family. In reviewing the literature, one comes on passage after passage by distinguished anthropologists who, unschooled in animal behavior, fail to recognize the significance. A characteristic response is that of Dr. M. F. Ashley Montagu, who in his popular volume *Man and Aggression* turned his arguments against the ethologists and the proposition that aggressiveness is innate in all species. He considered the ape's great canine tooth and concluded that it was for tearing apart tough forest fruits. Yet his conclusion quite neglected Washburn's evidence published almost ten years earlier.

In the same classic paper wherein Washburn presented his hunting hypothesis, he considered the problem of the primate's large canine tooth. Since food is not shared in any species of monkey or ape, and male or female face the same dietary challenge, males and females should have the same dental equipment. But they don't. The male chimpanzee's canine tooth is half again as long as the female's, the gorilla's twice as long, the rhesus monkey's two and a half times, and the savannah baboon's an appalling four times. Washburn concluded that the male canine dagger related not to food habits but to fighting. The exaggerated fighting tooth was either for display, within troop competition; for actual fighting for status; or for external defense of the troop against enemies.

Such neglect of evidence is a hallmark of halfway science. New York's famous psychiatrist Dr. Frederic Wertham has left his record in an inch or two of *Who's Who in the World*. His reputation has been established on his claim that comic strips and TV shows have taught our children to enjoy violence. None would dispute that violent behavior has been encouraged by such media. But Dr. Wertham has failed to consider that in America's Boston and Canada's Montreal young people get the same comic strips and the same TV shows, yet the rate of criminal violence in Boston exceeds that of Montreal by eight times. Likewise he has failed to consider that in the twelfth and thirteenth centuries, long before the printing press, let alone comic strips and TV, you could only with utmost courage step out of your house unarmed. One has only to live in Europe for a decade or two to recognize why, in Italy or Switzerland, medieval villages have been built with unbelievable effort on defensible hilltops. Lethal aggression has long predated TV shows.

This narrative is not primarily devoted to the problem of aggression. Yet the seductions of halfway science, exemplified by Montagu and Wertham, must intrude on it. You and I are considering the evolutionary origins of our nature, and we cannot be turned aside by the conclusions of those, whatever their public reputations, who must be regarded as anti-evolutionist. The reader is free to judge whether he goes along with Darwin or opposes him.

My presentation is Darwinian, yet much has happened to evolutionary thought since the time of Darwin. That is why I present the concept of cultural irreversibility. Natural selection proceeds as Darwin saw it. But once a cultural factor intrudes, such as the weapon, a biological consequence comes about, such as the loss of our fighting teeth. They became redundant, so that no pressure of natural selection was placed on their encouragement. Why had *Ramapithecus*, almost fifteen million years ago, tolerated the loss of large, fighting canines? Was it because a transfer had already been made to the weapon in the hand?

Such a conclusion, for lack of evidence, must be left until a time of future discovery. But this absence of fighting canines is a hallmark of hominid remains. Even though we can feel

45

in our own jawbones the vestigial roots of our long-lost fangs, still the tooth itself has been shrunken away for a very long time. Had we suffered such a loss of means to defend and assert ourselves in our true ape days, we should probably have not lived to maturity. But once the weapon entered our hands, our fighting teeth became of small survival necessity. So we became continuously dependent on it.

This is what I mean by cultural irreversibility. In the course of our long arboreal life we, like almost all primates, lost our claws. Now, through a long cultural life of transition on the ground, we lost our remaining natural weapons. Of necessity the weapon in the hand became a biological part of us, cultural though it might be described. We could not go back, whatever our wish.

And the weather continued to deteriorate.

The Pliocene Intervention

Five and a half million years ago the world was presented with a natural wonder which can rarely have been surpassed in our planet's long history. The Atlantic Ocean broke through a rocky barrier to form the Straits of Gibraltar and the Mediterranean Sea.

There have been other natural spectacles for which you and I were born too late. Two million years ago the massive volcano called Ngorongoro dominated the landscape of neighboring Olduvai Gorge, where some of our early ancestors were puttering about doing their best to provide us with a family tree. Its ashfalls and gases and lava flows made small contribution to their comfort, though—like the nuclear weapon—it was probably something you learned to live with. One day, however, it blew up, leaving a caldera—an immense dish-shaped hollow—of about one hundred square miles. It must have been a superior spectacle, although I find it difficult to believe that many spectators survived. Ngorongoro's caldera had the virtue, however, of presenting us with a permanent wonder, a natural game reserve much favored by tourists and scientists today.

What happened at the Straits of Gibraltar left us no legacy beyond the Mediterranean itself. Until a very few years ago, indeed, we had no scientific premonition that anything remarkable had happened at all. Then, in 1970, Kenneth Hsu, of Zurich, and several colleagues aboard the *Glomar Challenger* were cruising the Mediterranean indulging in that

47

newest of geology's delights, deep-sea drilling. Pioneered by oil companies ceaselessly searching for buried treasure, techniques and technologies now exist for exploring what lies beneath the sea bottom, a world we never knew. So Hsu and his friends were bringing up drill-cores from rocky deposits lying beneath six thousand feet of water. And there was something peculiar; they were coming on gravel.

Gravel occurs near shores, rarely at such depths. But then they came on the impossible, a mineral called anhydrite. It is an evaporite, a mineral that can come about only through the evaporation of shallow brines such as one finds in desert lakes, and only then at very high temperatures of almost one hundred degrees Fahrenheit. That the Mediterranean had once been a desert, or a scattering of pools like the Dead Sea, seemed preposterous. They pursued their investigations to depths of nine thousand feet, very nearly as deep as the Mediterranean gets, and came up with such deposits as stromatolites, which can form only in the presence of algae, which in turn can live only in near-surface water where sunlight can penetrate.

The entire Mediterranean had at one time resembled a leaky swimming pool from which all the water had drained away. How it had leaked away is not too difficult to understand if we recall the diminishing rainfall that had wiped out millions of square miles of Miocene forest. Even today Mediterranean waters evaporate far in excess of the contributions of such rivers as the Rhône and the Po and the Nile. Without the supplement of Atlantic waters rushing in past Gibraltar, the Mediterranean in a thousand years or so would eventually dry up and become again an enormous desert lying two miles below sea level.

Something had to give. About five and half million years ago, it gave. The Atlantic burst through the rocky wall that previously had blocked the Straits. Had it poured over the rim at the rate of a thousand cubic miles of water a year—

ten times the volume of Victoria Falls—the addition would have done no more than balance the evaporation of the Mediterranean deep. To fill it required a waterfall a hundred times bigger than Victoria, a thousand times larger than Niagara.

That is the natural wonder that we missed. At almost precisely the same date, we have the earliest known of the Kenya fossils: the hominid jaw from Lothagam Hill. It is unlikely that any of us wandered far enough to witness the most gigantic waterfall in history.

The Pliocene was in itself a natural wonder. It was that period of geological time following the abundant, though dwindling, Miocene and preceding the present Pleistocene, our time of unpredictable climatic swings between devouring continental ice sheets and such breathing spells as we enjoy today. Optimistic textbooks may label today's brief respite the *Holocene,* as if our troubles with glaciers were over. They are not. Our planet's weather has been deteriorating since the time of the ramapithecines, and presumably we have not seen the end of it.

Quite unlike the fickle Pleistocene, the African Pliocene was one of unremitting drought. If there were breathing spells, as there must have been—rains here or there, now and again—they left no record. Between Saldanha Bay, near the Cape of Good Hope, and northern Tanzania, from about ten million years ago until three million when, with the Pleistocene's first stirring, things began to look up, we have not a fossil bed. Presumably a few exist and have not yet been found, since Africa is large. Presumably life went on, somehow. But if life went on, death went uncommemorated. There was not enough water to convert bone into stone's immortality.

Yet this was the time and the place of the human emergence. When the long, dusty grip at last began to relax about three million years ago, we find ancestral man quite completely equipped in his skills and his anatomy, excepting only his still-small brain. How had we done it?

There is a very new clue. I have mentioned the recent analysis of Kenya as a region of tropical lowlands until about three million years ago, when the uplift began that gave us the present high, open plateau. In these same recent years two intrepid English geologists, W. W. Bishop and G. R. Chapman, made a search of the district lying west of Lake Rudolf. The great new hominid discoveries are to the east and north of the lake, reaching up into Ethiopia. It is along this line that, since about 1969, more remains of early man have been found than have been discovered in all the remainder of Africa since Raymond Dart made his original South African find in 1924. All reveal man emerging from the Pliocene. Yet it is about as formidable a piece of countryside as any the continent can propose, south of the Sahara. One region, to the west of Lake Rudolf, is worse—a piece of real estate that the moon would reject as unsuitable for astronauts.

Here Bishop and his colleague made their search. They found fossil bed after fossil bed, all Pliocene, some dating back as far as nine million years. Extinct antelope and giraffe, early hippos, wrote a fossil memoir in profusion. And it was in the midst of this forgotten graveyard, at Lothagam Hill, that at the time of the Gibraltar waterfall our first definite ancestor laid down his bones.

I repeat my surmise, supported by the new evidence, that in the Pliocene much of Kenya was a lowland. When the Miocene forests retreated, giving way to perhaps three million square miles of new grasslands, and when the great apes fell back to such sanctuaries as the Congo and perhaps West Africa, one pocket of relative affluence remained. Just how long it remained, we cannot yet say, but long enough for our transitional ancestors to gain a firm foothold on the new terrestrial life. Bishop reports lakes and streams and swamps.

In this limited area there was water enough to sustain not only our own lives, but the lives of those prey animals without which, as meat-eaters, we could not survive. The report explains our adaptation and survival in an impossible time, but perhaps it explains also why Kenya—and not Zambia or South Africa—became the metropolis of evolving man. However, I must make a considerable digression.

The hunting hypothesis rests on our necessity for meat which we ourselves hunted and killed. In Chapter One I described the death of the scavenger hypothesis as an alternative to the hunting proposal. We still face, however, the vegetarian hypothesis that we were never dependent on meat but rather on plant foods. The scavenger assumption has vanished through a variety of evidence piling up in the past five years. The vegetarian assumption has been placed in jeopardy by two quite independent investigations published in a single year, 1972.

In that year, in London, a book came out with a commonplace title, *What We Eat Today*. Since I have never myself seen it reviewed, I must assume that literary editors assigned it to the cookbook department. Yet in terms of nutrition—and by implication of our evolutionary origins too—it is revolutionary. The book was written by Michael Crawford and his wife Sheila, largely out of his experience as head of biochemistry at Britain's respected Nuffield Institute of Comparative Medicine, but also after long field research in East Africa. His conclusions stunned me. I wrote to him expressing my consequent suspicion that the significant expansion of the ape brain could have occurred only in a meat-eating animal. I found my suspicion confirmed.

Much of Dr. Crawford's emphasis lies on the importance of fats. Biochemistry is not an easy subject, and to complicate matters in our time fats have become a bad word. But there are two kinds, it seems, the visible and the invisible. Visible fats are those that a woman stores on her thighs, a man on his paunch, an overfed steer in his marbled meat. These are the saturated fats that we are warned against. But there are invisible, structural fats essential to the normal growth of cells, and in particular to the growth of those nerve cells that congregate in our brain.

These fatty acids, as biochemists call them, constitute by dry weight about 50 percent of our central nervous system—our brain, our spinal cord, and our proliferating nerves—and of the walls of our blood vessels as well. Normal development cannot come about without them. Like almost all foods, the fatty acids originate in plants, but they are of simple order. There are two general sorts: linoleic, which appears mostly in seeds, and linolenic, characteristic of such greens as grass. Only animals can convert them into the elongated chains which we need for our nervous and vascular systems. Herbivores do it, and in the course of a season they convert first the linolenic from grass, later the linoleic from ripening seeds, storing up both. Yet the herbivore remains an intermediary, for it is a very slow process to convert the longer fatty chains that do not exist in the plant world into the highly elongated chains that we need for our central nervous systems. It is also the intermediary in that the chains it produces, while necessary, are still too simple.

That is where the carnivore comes in. He profits by the herbivore's season of storage with a single kill and a single meal. Furthermore, from the simpler chains of the browsing or grazing animals, it can produce as a next step in the food chain the building blocks—the long, complex cells that our neural and vascular systems demand. No large-brained being need be exclusively a meat-eater. Crawford recognizes the value of vegetable proteins, but emphasizes that "the real value in animal products may well lie in the fact that they also supply a spectrum of structural fats not found in vegetation." To the potential dismay of our hungry world, he points out that soybeans and peanuts, while rich in protein, contain no structural fats at all. But for the encouragement of nursing mothers, he adds that human milk is rich in structural fats, whereas in cow's milk they are scarcely detectable. That our relative brain size is fifty times that of the cow, may of course be a coincidence.

Michael Crawford's iconoclastic research cannot by itself define evolving man as a consistent meat-eater, but other evidence was appearing from odd corners of thought. In 1972, the same year that his book appeared, Professor A. Carl Leopold and I published in *Science* a paper called "Toxic Substances in Plants and Food Habits of Early Man." Two years earlier, in *The Social Contract*, I had suggested that the vegetarian hypothesis was a fallacy. It is true that most contemporary hunting peoples gather quantities of plant food—but all have fire. In anthropology we had not only come to use the term *hunters-and-gatherers*, to describe these peoples, but we had projected it far into our evolutionary past. There are only a few plant foods of any caloric value, however, that we can digest without cooking. There are nuts, of course, certain oily seeds such as sunflower and sesame, a few edible roots and shoots, and wild honey in its short season. And of course there were greens on the grasslands, beyond number, but virtually lacking in caloric content. Nor can we, like horses, live off grass. Even to digest leaves in quantity requires in our primate family the highly specialized stomachs of the colobus and langur. Without doubt we could have lived off fruit as does the chimp, but there is not a hominid site in all of Pleistocene Africa that at the time of our occupation indicates forests extensive enough to have provided us with a steady fruit supply. As few deny, we were savannah beings.

The vegetarian hypothesis amounts very nearly to scripture in American anthropology. It received strong, if temporary, reinforcement by way of a proposition advanced by Clifford Jolly that our adaptation to grassland life was made not by meat-eating but by seed-eating. The proposition seemed persuasive, since seeds could provide the calories that greens could not, and they would be present everywhere. That seeds form a most inconspicuous portion of the traditional ape diet presents no difficulty, since meat provides even less. There even exists a precedent in such seed-eating monkeys as the gelada in the northern Ethiopian grasslands. Seeds have provided their means of survival without forest fruits. Another startling precedent existed in the person of *Gigantopithecus*, the monstrous Asian ape, now extinct, who seems definitely to have made his adaptation to the Pliocene savannahs by means of a diet of seeds.

But there are problems. There is the matter of dentition. While *Gigantopithecus*, like the hominid, had small canine teeth, still, according to David Pilbeam, Yale's authority on dentition, they were heavy grinders resembling not at all our chisel-like slicers. And though the northern grassland monkeys faced the same defensive necessity against predators, seed-eating is a sedentary occupation. None evolved the least tendency towards running feet and erect posture. And there was another problem: if eating grass seeds had entered at any time our ancestral heritage, why is it that we can't eat them uncooked?

Cooking and the control of fire are recent inventions. This was the element in anthropology's conventional wisdom that so disturbed me in *The Social Contract*. None of our vegetable staffs of life—our wheat, our rice, our maize, our beans—can be eaten raw in any quantity at all without remarkable digestive uproar. I knew little about the subject beyond wondering what my neighbors, the Italians, would have done had they founded a culture on uncooked spaghetti. But my readers happen frequently to be my most remarkable contributors, and I received a letter from Carl Leopold, professor of plant physiology at Purdue University. He suggested that I might be unaware of how large a subject I had opened.

Through long processes of evolution, plants have entered a prey-predator relationship with animals. Some, like many seeds and roots and berries, are equipped with chemical repellants to discourage animal consumption. Others, taking a trickier approach, boast attractants such as perfume or flavor or color that will induce you to eat them. The seeds, however, being indigestible, will be defecated elsewhere, thus nobly contributing to the evolutionary ends of reproduction.

Few anthropologists know anything about plant physiology; few plant physiologists know very much about anthropology. So, as a result of our original correspondence, we collaborated on the paper that *Science* published on May 5, 1972. We raised no rebel flags but simply demonstrated what an evolutionary breakthrough had come about for evolving man when, with the invention of controlled fire, we learned through cooking to disarm the repellants. A world of plant food became available.

There were so many things I had never known: for example, that beans and the whole legume family, when ripened, incorporate with their richness of protein and starch a repellant called *protease.* Any housewife can testify just how many hours beans must be cooked if her family is not to be corroded by acidity. It is the protease that must be broken down through the oxidation of cooking.

I did not know that there are roots even more menacing. Yams and manioc—in some places called cassava—are staples without which many a tropical population would find existence difficult. Raw yams come equipped with enzymes so strong as to throw all our metabolism out of gear. (Cultivation of yams in Mexico has become a major industry of late, since it is these enzymes that furnish the basic ingredient for The Pill.) Manioc takes the course of including with its starches a pleasant dose of cyanide. The heat that dispels the legume's protease, or the yam's enzymes, likewise oxidizes the manioc's cyanide. The same effect can be produced in manioc by prolonged pounding and exposure to air. But archaeologists have found no Stone Age artifact designed for pounding plant food.

My original concern had been with cereals—those starchy, high-calorie seeds that we began to domesticate from wild grasses about ten thousand years ago, and that today provide most of mankind with energy. Why do I bother with the grinding of flour and the baking of bread? Why do I eat my rice boiled, my barley in soup, my oats in porridge, my rye in pumpernickel? Well, there is an excellent reason: because the seed, taken in any quantity at all, is inedible. The macromolecule of starch is far too large for our digestive fluids to break down. Heat splits it. Most grains can be fermented, it is true, but again we come to archaeology. While in earlier times we must have made use of animal skins, until we come down to pottery we had no true containers for the fermenting process. And the oldest known pottery was made at Çatal Hüyük, in Turkey, about 6800 B.C.—not very long ago.

Cooking, and only cooking, made available to us the world of high-calorie plant food on which we depend today. The techniques of cooking obviously depended on our control of fire. We tend to forget, as we equate the ways of contemporary relic peoples with the ways of ancestral man, the recency of that invention. Not until 300,000 or 400,000 years ago did we even begin to appreciate fire's value. *Homo erectus,* with his half-expanded brain, has left us occasional hearths from Choukuotien to the mouth of the Rhône, and seems to have used fire for rounding up game in Spain. Yet significantly, at that date, we find no evidence in warm Africa. Cold Eurasia, in all likelihood, placed a value on fire for its heat. Certainly, beyond roasted bones, there remains no evidence for cooking. Also, it is generally believed that *Homo erectus* didn't know how to make fire but instead relied on collecting it from grass fires or lightning-struck trees.

When we come down to Neanderthal, beginning about

56

100,000 years ago, hearths are common, yet still sporadic. They are still unknown in Africa and rare in the Middle East. Only at the time of Cro-Magnon man's entry into Europe, about thirty-five thousand years ago, do we find hearths universal not only in Europe but throughout all the Old World. In the opinion of Oakley, our accepted authority, some simple technique for making fire—perhaps the striking of flint against iron pyrite to produce incendiary sparks—had by then been invented. Truly controlled fire, a necessity for dependence on cooking, had at last come about.

Evolving man, from those distant times when he renounced the abundance and the security of the forest, could have survived only as an opportunist. We satisfied our hunger with whatever we could find, catch, and digest. If there were nuts to be gathered, we gathered nuts. When berries ripened we ate berries. If locusts swarmed, then we joined in a protein scramble, and when wild honey came into its short season, we reveled in honey and ignored the bee stings. We were omnivores, and any portrait of evolving man as exclusively carnivorous would be false. Yet far more fallacious is the popular vision of ancestral women and children spread out through the fields and the bush gathering our necessary vegetables, while the men went hunting for the fun of it. Until controlled fire came to our rescue, we ate meat because we had to.

A remarkable correlation between our use of fire and our consumption of plant foods was published in *Scientific American* as recently as January, 1975. It was a study of human coprolites. The work was started by a Canadian, Eric Callen, in the 1960's and is today being pursued by several laboratories. Coprolites are the desiccated or petrified remains of feces. The feces of animal species are usually quite distinctive. In ancient faunal assemblages they can sometimes tell us much about the comings and goings of such creatures as hyenas. Back in the days when most authorities

57

regarded Raymond Dart's vast accumulation of 500,000 fossil bones at the Makapan site as the work of hyenas, a striking line of proof favoring occupancy by hominids was the rarity of hyena feces.

So coprolites can contribute much information, but not until Callen had human remains been systematically studied. His subjects came from old American Indian deposits, and analysis of their contents revealed just about everything from bird feathers to eggshells, but most significantly the remains of plant fibers and seeds. So perfectly were they preserved in the coprolites that one could judge from Mexican sites whether millet seeds had been crushed, indicating preparation by pounding, or split, probably by rolling in a stone *metate* just as is done today. Dependence on plant food was everywhere indicated. But there is a catch. The Indian migration to America came so late that all knew the techniques of fire-making, all had hearths, and all had cooking. Earlier Pleistocene remains from Europe tell a different story.

Admittedly the Neanderthal coprolites studied so far have been too few for firm conclusions, but they showed no plant remains whatsoever. Their age is about fifty thousand years, before widespread use of controlled fire. A Texas laboratory is now studying a few larger samples of about five hundred coprolites found by Henry de Lumley at the much older site of Terra Amata on the French Riviera. And no plant remains have been found.

Placed against such accumulating evidence, the vegetarian hypothesis falters. Yet still another point emerges. The Pleistocene coprolites being studied come of course from Ice Age Europe, where for the last half-million years we seem to have climaxed our evolution. And we fail to consider what the climate must have been—the interminable winters, the swift, cool summers. Where did we gather our plant foods in winter? There were none. It was hunt and eat meat, or perish. Yet a fascinating question arises. In milder climates we had greens, which despite their lack of calories could provide our Vitamin C. But what about Vitamin C when, through the long Ice Age winters, our diet could have consisted of little but meat?

There is an answer, and it came to us a long time ago. Lack of fruit and vegetables, and the consequent vitamin-deficiency disease called scurvy, had dogged shipmasters for as long as we took long voyages. British ships took to stocking limes for such voyages, so that the term *limey* has stuck to British sailors to this day. But early in this century the Icelandic but Canadian-born Arctic explorer, Vilhjalmur Stefansson, spent five continuous years north of the Arctic circle living precisely in the manner of his Eskimo companions. Eight months of that time they never touched land, lived on drifting ice floes, hunted seals, and ate nothing but meat. They suffered no damage, having eaten it raw. And so Stefansson's contribution to the hunting hypothesis was the conclusion that meat lacks nothing in Vitamin C, provided that you do not cook it.

I have little doubt that the phrase *hunters and gatherers* will continue to pervade anthropology's literature. To a limited degree it is correct, since as evolving opportunists we ate whatever we could gather and digest. Yet the vegetarian hypothesis, like the scavenger hypothesis, is a fallacy. We were never exclusively carnivorous, any more than we are today. But if Leopold and the plant physiologists are correct, then the high-calorie plant foods which we can today substitute for meat were unavailable before cooking. If Crawford is correct, then only by means of the fatty acids contained in meat could the nine thousand million neurones of our brain have evolved. And if our knowledge of the Ice Age is correct, then we were beings long preadapted throughout our equatorial experience to survive frozen winters of unimaginable duration when we lived off meat alone.

Yet for many reasons, bad or good, we shall continue to reject the thesis that man is man, and has survived to this date, because we killed for a living. We shall reject it because its acceptance would demand the rewriting of too many textbooks. We shall reject it because anthropology—the study of man—has become all too frequently the mere study of contemporary primitive people, while we forget that the past is not the present. (Claude Lévi-Strauss, in a lecture at the Smithsonian Institution in September, 1965, bemoaned the coming extinction of anthropology, since soon there would be no more primitive people to study.) We shall reject the thesis because of the authority of such well-written studies as Richard Lee's examination of a Bushman hunting society, in which meat contributes but 33 percent of their diet. That they were most unrepresentative Bushmen, living a sedentary existence around water holes; that in the neighborhood there was an enormous mongongo-nut forest providing an ample, rich, easily gathered food supply; that, in truth, of their daily intake of 2,140 calories only 190 were derived from plant foods other than nuts—such reservations are easily forgotten, particularly if forgetting is what we wish.

Supreme, above all other reasons for rejecting the hunting hypothesis, is anthropology's will to believe in primal man happily, healthily chewing his mongongo nuts. Such an anthropological wonder can bear comparison only to the one-time waterfall at Gibraltar. Just as wonderful, in a century as catastrophic as our own, is the Rousseauesque image of primal innocence, primal goodness, that grips our minds. Yet perhaps the wonder is not too great. A Shakespeare or a Goethe, in days less dark, could look at man's nature without blinking. For the decent young man today, condemned as by a life sentence to survive somehow the next half-century, it is far easier, hope against hope, to embrace a philosophy of original decency. He does not want to hear, and I do not blame him, that we are human beings because for millions of years we killed for a living.

The irony is profound. Were we the descendants of beings who through that same long, demonstrable time-span scrounged for a living as does the baboon today—digging a root here, coming on a fortunate ripening of palm nuts there, turning over rocks for edible scorpions, strangling a fawn when a fawn came our way—then of course we should not face a future beyond baboon conception or baboon solution. Or were we the descendants of fruit-dependent chimpanzees locked into their shrinking forests, then naturally we should have no future problems at all beyond extinction. It is *because* we were hunters, *because* we killed for a living, *because* we matched our wits against the whole of the animal world, that we have the wit to survive even a world of our own creation.

But the irony extends far beyond the evolution of primate wit. Had we remained the gatherers of plant food that so many of our wishful thinkers demand, then we should never have progressed beyond the normal primate existence in which no one feeds another, neither male nor female nor child. We may today neglect our responsibilities; still, responsibility remains a human norm. We may refuse to cooperate, yet cooperation still regularly invests us as it seldom invests the ape. Willingness to forego self-interest, even to sacrifice oneself for some larger good, may reach the vanishing point in times of human panic and confusion, but the willingness is there, a human endowment, and it can emerge whenever the danger signal rings clear. Our amiable, fruit-eating cousin will not even give a signal of warning until he has safely hidden himself.

And there is a final irony. At an hour quite desperate in terms of any intelligent estimate of future survival—at an hour so confused by so many threats to our existence that we cannot put our minds without distraction on any one of them—at an hour when I myself sometimes give way to the ultimate depression, the conviction that at last human accomplishment has outrun the powers of human direction—our temptation must be to find refuge in nostalgia, in romance, in a remembrance of things past that never were. Only by turning our remorseless backs on such temptation, only by seeking the reality of a human past that still invests us, can we discover the origins of those characters of courage and cooperation, of ingenuity and wit, of cunning and adaptability, of affection and human bonding, that without our hunting past would have been a natural impossibility.

I sometimes wonder whether without the intervention of that natural accident, the African Pliocene drought, there could be people.

The first consequence of the African Pliocene and the withdrawal of forest was the slow change in the human foot. I have described the beginnings of our bipedal locomotion, the freeing of our hands, our dependence on the weapon in the hand. I have described that irreversible hour in our evolution—an hour undoubtedly millions of years long—when our long fighting canine teeth became no longer of selective value for our survival and so became reduced to the hominid's size and our own. Dependence on the weapon in the hand—our first adventure into culture—had its biological consequences, the discard of our only remaining natural weapon. We could not go back. We were dependent on the cultural weapon in the hand.

Whenever it was—just how early in the Pliocene—that we became dependent on hunting for survival, a second irreversible biological change came about. It is true that despite our small size and our awkwardness on the ground, the earliest hunting may have been quite easy. We had precisely the same advantage that Paul Martin has described when the early hunters reached America from Asia. Prey animals were innocent. They were wary of the saber-tooth, of other large ancestral cats, of the flourishing hyena, but they had no more reason to fear us than a mixed herd of impala and zebra has reason to fear baboons today. In another of Kortlandt's phrases, the early savannah must have been a butcher's paradise. But this paradise, like others, had its own way of getting lost. The game became wary.

In any prey-predator relationship there is a reciprocal evolution: the one develops a better means of defense, while the other must develop means of penetrating it. Neither is independent of the ways and weaknesses of the other. One of the most successful—and hilarious—means of defense that has ever come to my attention is that of the larva of a beetle called *Cassida rubiginosa,* whose natural enemy is a predatory ant. For a long time zoologists groped for the selective value of a trash packet that the larva carries on its back as it crawls along. A two-pronged fork rises from the tip of the larva's abdomen, catching successively molted skins to form a kind of tray. Anatomically the feature is odd enough, but it is combined with an anal tunnel that rises to deposit fecal matter in the packet. A solution was finally found in the temperament of the ant, whose weakness is a fastidious nature. When the ant approaches and gives its prey a preliminary feel, the larva goes into action with its trayful of unpleasantness, splattering the ant. The fastidious predator has no choice but to fall back and clean up, while the larva goes its way. The device is known as a fecal shield.

The competition on the ancient savannah, to begin with at least, was less ingenious. As game became alert to our presence, the handlike foot of our ape ancestry would no longer do. Undoubtedly, in the course of our bipedal pre-adaptation, our feet improved to a degree. But these were days when the need to climb trees, whether for food or protection, was still part of our life. Our terrestrial adventures meant getting around sufficiently erect to free our hands and to hold a weapon, but not to surrender our trees. Now came the need to run.

Bishop's discovery of a Pliocene region in Kenya that preserved for some millions of years an environment not too rig-

63

orous has relieved me of a worry that has been hanging over my studies for a very long time. The adaptation of the human foot to the running demands of the hunting life has been far and away more complex than the *Cassida* larva's fecal shield. Not just the flattening to conform with the flat earth, but the development of an arch to give spring to our steps and even of the crosswise metatarsal arch allowing the pressure of our toes for balance and for a grip on the earth, are adaptations that could have come about only through millions of years of continuing selection.

The human foot is a biological consequence of the hunting culture that could never have come about in creatures dependent on plant food. While it might be argued that flight from predators would provide selective advantage sufficient to promote its evolution, we must recall the seed-eaters of the northern savannahs. The male patas monkey is by far the fastest of all primates. Yet he, the gelada, and the hamadryas all faced the same predators as we did, and none developed anything but the normal primate foot. The cost was too great. The foot that could pursue game across grasslands could no longer scurry up a tree. Unlike that dilettante hunter, the chimpanzee, or that occasional, seasonal hunter, the common baboon, neither of which ever sacrificed the grasping foot and the security of trees, an evolutionary moment had to come for the evolving hominid when his life became more dependent on the successful kill than the secure escape.

The existence of environments in which such an evolutionary moment could have stretched out over countless evolving years fills a needed gap in the human story. We know from John Napier's superb studies of foot-bones almost two million years old, from lower Olduvai, that by then the foot had very nearly—though not quite—completed its evolution. We know from the straight leg-bones of Richard Leakey's East Rudolf man, almost three million years old, that

64

the feet supporting them must have achieved equivalent merit. And finally—at least tentatively as of this date—we know from Johanson's Ethiopian discoveries, still older, that leg-bones indicate no striking deficiency of feet. The commitment to terrestrial life had taken place long before.

But what a commitment it was, psychical as well as anatomical. The renunciation of the trees meant a reversal of primate psychology: we could flee only so far and so fast; then we had to fight. The commonplace question, How can man be innately aggressive when the chimpanzee is not? has run into the problem, as we have discovered, that the chimp is not quite as nonaggressive a creature as we once assumed. But the large answer to the question lies, of course, in the terrestrial adventure and our renunciation of the forest. Just as an airliner on take-off passes that point of no return when it must fly or crash, so we passed a point of no return in our commitment to the ancient, hazardous savannah. We would survive here, or we would die here. We could never go back.

Even as in our inspection of those qualities of preadaptation without which the human potential would have been impossible, we found the syndrome of bipedal locomotion, freed hands, and the expedient weapon: so at this later evolutionary moment we find a syndrome of qualities that have emerged inextricably tied. Which came first one may guess, but it does not matter. All were basically human, all were new to the primate, all had to succeed or the new being would fail.

Of first importance, I should speculate, was cooperation. It was as if this entirely new being, having sacrificed the primate stronghold of the trees, had to invent a substitute stronghold. And for a primate, it *was* an invention. Cooperation between a few individuals may occur briefly in a chimpanzee hunt, but it vanishes with the division of the spoils. Two rhesus monkeys may form a temporary political coalition against a joint rival. Various territorial species, like the vervet, may join the efforts of a band to resist invasion of its private real estate; when the invader is repelled, cooperation ceases. The three or four alpha baboons will enforce law and order within the troop, combine their fangs against an external enemy, and remain allies. They are an exception.

But all these forms of cooperation are relatively simple as compared with that of the wolf pack or the lion pride. A continuing pursuit of a common objective on the part of a group has little primate precedent. But it is a paramount characteristic of the social predator.

As I have discussed, the sharing of food after the age of weaning, excepting only the sharing of meat after a chimpanzee hunt, is unknown among primate species. But the renunciation of the forest and its fruit meant the end of easy food supply for mothers and young. They had to be fed. With what zeal our early male hunters accepted the role of food-provider, I do not know. But there was nothing revolutionary about it if you were a social predator.

The primate is a footloose creature possessing nothing resembling a daytime home. The chacma baboons may return to favorite sleeping trees or cliffs, the hamadryas to the safety of rocks and numbers. The arboreal gibbon pair or callicebus monkey may favor some sleeping limb through simple habituation, but with the morning they are gone. The concept of the home as the focus for a social group of mixed ages and mixed sexes as other than a nocturnal refuge finds no indication in the history of apes and monkeys. Yet even the mysterious ramapithecines of Miocene forest days had their evident living site, differing not at all from the Olduvai sites a mere two million years old.

The home was as new an idea for the hunting primate as cooperative action itself, or male responsibility for basic food. Our young matured slowly. Away from the security of the trees, we combined the biological disadvantages of the ape with the predatory hazards of life in the open. There had to be a place for the care and defense of our helpless young by day as well as night, so, just as the male sacrificed his carefree, roaming life, females sacrificed their own independence to the security of the home-place. But while such a semipermanent institution might be new to the vegetarian primate, there was nothing new about it to the predator. We have even taken from his ways certain terms in our language, such as *den* and *lair*.

One more quality, which I have mentioned but fleetingly, must have been a portion of that early syndrome. Loosely we call it courage. It is a bundle of qualities in itself: willingness to dare, to persevere, to respond to challenge by attack rather than escape. It is the capacity to make judgments and take risks, to try what one has not tried before. It is frequently to inhibit one's most profound instinct for personal survival in the interest of larger values; frequently to defer one's personal inclinations to the judgment of another who one has reason to believe knows better; to be loyal; to accept with at least moderate equanimity self-sacrifice as the price of species survival, even though one has never given it much thought. Loosely, I say this is courage, and we should never have survived the Pliocene without it. I must add, loosely again since exceptions are notable, that such courage is less the quality of the primate than of the cooperating social predator.

I hope that without too great resort to italics and capital letters I have sufficiently emphasized that basic elements of our nature which we regard as human—even nobly and uniquely human—came into being not because we were fruit-eating apes, but because we were meat-eating hunters. Yet a decade or two ago such a proposal would have been wild indeed.

Fortunately for the human investigator, since about 1960 the sciences have been receiving not only the massive discoveries of our paleontologists, filling in and extending the knowledge of our fossil past; not only the discoveries of physicists and chemists, providing us with new and accurate means of ancient dating, which combined with the paleobotanist's patient studies of fossil pollens present us with portraits of ancient climates and landscapes; not only the meteoric advances in molecular genetics and the mechanics of inheritance, giving us for the first time a comprehension of how the past is a portion of the present; not only from the ethologists such massive observations of primate behavior in the wild that what were inspired guesses a decade ago can now be inspected with statistical care; but also, in the short time since 1970, all of our major studies of the great carnivores, our competitors in ages past.

In the winter just preceding the beginnings of this windfall, George Schaller and Geoffrey Lowther published a brief paper (the one in which they tested the hominid capacity to survive as a scavenger) stating clearly the thesis that had been bothering African specialists ever since Dart published his *Predatory Transition from Ape to Man.* In biological language the thesis was this: whatever the phylogeny of the human being (in other words, its zoological inheritance from the primate family), what could not be neglected was the ecological separation of man and ape for millions of years yet unknown. To translate:

Darwinian evolution postulates that within a given environment there will be differences in the capacity of individuals to bring their offspring to reproductive maturity. This is natural selection—"the survival of the fittest"—as evolutionists see it today. It resembles not at all the jungle law that fascinated and horrified the Victorians. In no manner does it resemble Tennyson's "nature red in tooth and claw." The meek may well inherit the earth if they leave sufficient offspring—and provide an earth in which the offspring can survive.

The catch-phrase is "in a given environment." What hap-

68

pened to us in our Pliocene experience was that when our evolving foot renounced the retreating trees and we made the irreversible commitment to a terrestrial hunting life for survival necessity, we accepted a new environment. We accepted natural selection as imposed by the commandments of the savannah, of an order quite different from that of forest benevolence. And a radically new environment meant that we lived or died, reproduced successfully or not, became extant or extinct, according to a radically new code of environmental rules.

There follows a challenge to any present understanding of man. We must see him not just in terms of primate inheritance, but in terms of his successful survival as a hunter for millions upon millions of years. Illuminating though such studies may be, it is not enough to study the ape except in terms of primate potential; we must study man also as a social predator, since that is what we became. And until recently such investigation has been difficult.

We lacked an authoritative literature. In 1967 George Schaller came back from India with *The Deer and the Tiger,* but there had been far fewer tigers than deer. Then at last came David Mech's long-awaited study of the wolf, a true social predator. In the same year, 1970, the van Lawick-Goodall workshop published its collaborative *Innocent Killers,* and two years later came the classic pair, George B. Schaller's *The Serengeti Lion* and Hans Kruuk's *The Spotted Hyena.* Schaller's intensive three-year experience had covered not only the lion but the cheetah, the leopard, and that most significant social killer, the African hunting dog. Kruuk's even longer study revealed the hyena as not just the scavenger that even Herodotus had recorded, but a pack-hunter and perhaps the second most formidable predator on the savannah. In the midst of the rush of publications came Goodall's perfect counterpoint, *In the Shadow of Man,* recording her ten-year experience with the wild chimpanzee.

For any present student of man the combined works were a treasury. The careful assessment of prey by the wolf, weighing its strength against vulnerabilities; the tactical hunting of lionesses setting an ambush here, diverting the prey's attention there; the intensive cooperation of the hunting dog, compensating as man must once have done for individual vulnerability; the inexplicable resolve of the hyena pack, setting out on a hunt, to pursue one species of prey and ignore all others—all are discoveries illuminating the capacity of the far-brainier hominid, even in his earliest savannah days, to hunt successfully. Yet they are such recent discoveries that the sciences of man have had little time to digest them. However, digest them we must, for science is a process. Like a sea it swells up from the deep to deposit on old beaches new margins of novel shells, novel stones, that we never knew before. Science as a process can never stand still, never rest on perpetuating dogmas, but, as in any other region of human experience, must adapt itself continually to new terrains of discovery.

We may, of course, turn our backs on science and—rejecting all evidences, all discoveries, all logical courses as irrelevant to the human presence—turn our meandering thoughts to the occult, to the conjoining of planets, to the splendid interventions of extraterrestrial beings. Yet even as we lost our fangs in the course of our cultural evolution and could not go back; even as we lost our climbing feet on the flat savannah and could never return to our forest security; even as at a much later date we evolved our enlarged brain with all its perceptive, analytical, self-questioning processes (and its faults as well)—I find it difficult to believe that we can ever as a species return to the animism of Disneylike threatening trees, favorable omens, unfavorable ghosts, and far-placed stars influencing your life or mine.

Perhaps all is a matter of preference. If so, science is mine. Never will it teach us all we need to know. Never will it provide us with final answers, and since none exist, then science's weakness becomes science's strength. Never will it cease its controversies, and that too is just as well if truth, like infinity, is to be eternally sought, though never captured. So it is that I must prefer the informed to the convinced, the demonstrated to the revealed, the observed to the imagined, the probable to the impossible, the unalterable fact to the evanescent wish, the reasoned conclusion—however offensive —to the unquestioned assumption—however pleasing. And so I restate my original proposition:

Our humanity is not the consequence but the cause of our becoming human beings.

In its most fundamental terms, our humanity evolved on the unending savannahs of the African Pliocene. The most basic characteristics of man existed in an ugly little being whom we should never have invited home to dinner. Small-brained, physically inadequate, we could never have survived for a generation, let alone for a time that only stars can measure, had we not been perfecting those qualities that we regard as so nobly our own: sharing, cooperation, responsibility, courage, self-sacrifice, loyalty.

I restate my wonder as to whether, without the trials of the African Pliocene—an accident of nature—there could ever have been people. Again my mind goes back to those remarkable ramapithecines of the ancient, abundant Miocene. If they failed, as did their Indian cousins, could their failure not be attributed to the lack of an environment so harsh as to be intolerant of compromise? No such lack came about with the Pliocene.

Finally, I have suggested that the qualities that we so rightfully admire in *Homo sapiens* have come to us less through our primate inheritance of expanding intelligence, and more through our evolution as social predators. It is a touchy point, since so often our primate intelligence is in conflict with our predatory inclinations. But it is the story of this book. So I must proceed with my investigation of why we are not chimpanzees, and I must proceed without mercy, as my primate intelligence and my predatory curiosity demand.

The Sexual Adventure

We do not hold our sexuality in proper reverence. It is a human invention unique in the world of living things. I cannot believe that in all our splendid catalogue of invention—washing machines, windshield-wipers, defoliants, the flush toilet, the internal combustion engine, French champagne, jet travel, the safety pin, the Christmas tree, napalm, fish and chips—any has brought quite so much satisfaction to quite so many members of our species with a generosity quite so fair-handed. I can't say whether the robin envies our overwhelming brain, but if it does not envy us our unique sexuality, then it is a most unimaginative bird. And it was the evolving human female who dreamed it up.

Before the human emergence the natural history of sex, granted a bizarre deviation or two, is on the whole a dreary one. Those among us who would condemn certain of our actions as bestial are giving the animal far more credit than is its due. I find it a matter of some disapproval that through hundreds of millions of evolving years natural selection gave such encouragement to improvements in swimming, or air-breathing, or climbing or flying or subtle navigational aids to migration and homing, and paid so little attention to sex. Perhaps the idea was so good in the first place that no selective pressure was placed on improving it.

To begin with, no doubt, the idea of sexual reproduction was a masterstroke. Life had survived its billions of monotonous Pre-Cambrian years dominated by essentially immortal

73

single-celled beings who reproduced through division. It was good enough, in a way, and perhaps it had to be slow to develop such universal accoutrements of life as the DNA code and the cell itself, and the will to survive. Yet what could be duller, less challenging, more predictable than two daughters produced by division who could not be unlike you, since they *were* you?

Sex turned everything topsy-turvy. With the basic idea of producing one fairly unpredictable offspring from the union of two genetically differing parents, natural selection got what it wanted. Infinite diversity meant infinite selective choice. Gone were the drowsy days of identical twins, and the nights of the protozoa.

Sex was the key, five million years ago, that unlocked a biological future of proliferating species and rapid adaptation to new environments. But the animal might well complain. Having got what it wanted, natural selection tolerated some of the dullest means of procreation ever to enter the evolutionary record. I do not deny that a few early experiments hold a fascination. There is something most attractive about a pair of octopuses gently feeling each other with all sixteen arms. The human being may regret his anatomical limitations. Yet octopus consummation falls quite flat compared to the build-up. Similarly, the spectacular sexual invasion of a California beach by the Pacific fish, the grunion, whose male will gyrate for female excitement, might be regarded as getting somewhere. But in the end the female will simply lay her eggs in the sand in old fish-fashion, and he will fertilize them. And the ungainly dances of the ostrich cock, the ingenious constructions of the New Guinea bowerbird, the attentive feeding of his fiancée by the European jackdaw, are all build-ups to a let-down. Amazing elaborations of the décor of sex may have come about, but it is the same old furniture. Certain species of insects like spiders and the praying mantis, in which the female has a hearty appetite

74

for the male as a table delicacy, have admittedly introduced a flourish to the sexual act itself. There is always the suspense as to whether she will eat him before or afterward, and even the outside chance that he will get away with it.

A few animal adventures with sex have had their entertainment value, but they have largely been sideshows. The problem seems to have been that natural selection has been concerned only with results. If you are a salmon, as the breeding season comes on you may accomplish miracles of navigation in the open sea to reach a certain river, and you will endure untold hardships of upriver struggle to reach an ordained little brook. But when you have reached it, then she will unloose her eggs in some shallow spot and he will cloud the waters with sperm, and that will be that. So long as we still get poached salmon for lunch, nature will have done her duty.

Reproduction, not sex, is the essential criterion for species' success or failure. As I have cited in another book, Sir Arthur Keith once wrote that child-raising is the first industry of every species, and if that industry fails, then the species becomes extinct. Natural selection takes place among diverse offspring, and so long as sexual reproduction provides those offspring, what selective pressure can come about to improve the system? It is a point to keep in mind as we approach the innovations of human sexuality, since they would never have come about had old conservative systems worked.

To return to my cavalier treatment, a new sexual idea did not come about until perhaps 200 million years ago, when we were reptiles. The male contributed the penis. So far as I know, it was the last contribution that the unimaginative male ever made. And what happened to it? Descendant birds —except for a few pioneering species like the ostrich—forgot about it. The regrettable oversight inspired David Lack, whose study of Galapagos finches I have described, to comment on the Freudian proposition that we fear snakes because they resemble the penis. Birds are terrified by snakes, Lack acidly recorded, yet they have no penis at all.

I can think of no greater waste of time and energy than the sex life of birds. For all such elaborations of courtship as I have mentioned, for all the displays of the peacock or the bird of paradise, for all the antiphonal singing of a pair of East African bou-bou shrikes, when the great moment comes she hunches over, he mounts her, briefly they rub their cloacas together, and it is all over.

Fortunately for the natural history of sex, when the mammal descended from a different reptile line the male remembered his penis. This tiny, arboreal, insect-eating creature, the ancestral mammal of a hundred million years ago, was a truly revolutionary animal with his new dental arrangements, his fur and internal heating system, and his rudimentary cortex with potentially superior capacities for learning. In one feature of the revolution, child care, he resembled the birds. The reptile's normal concern for offspring was simply to bury eggs in a hole and forget about them. While the transaction may have a certain contemporary appeal, still old Cretaceous fossil beds are rich with the remains of extinct reptiles. Perhaps so long as the reptile way lacked competition it was good enough, but while the bird continued to lay eggs, the mother took devoted care of nestlings and scored the huge evolutionary success that still delights us. The mammal, with its internal gestation and external feeding equipment, scored an even bigger success, for which we as inheritors may be grateful.

Granting that the young were to be conceived within the mother's body, retention of the reptile penis by the mammal male seems more likely a matter of anatomical necessity than one of conserving his assets. So far as any brilliant contribution to sex may be judged, the mammal male might still be back in the late Permian. If you watch lizards and lions copulating, then you will see that in 200 million years the male has had not a single new idea. He still approaches her from the rear, probably grasps her neck in his teeth, and has done with it in short order. Even if in subdued awe you witness the sexual endurance of the male lion in an African game reserve, you must recognize that the prowess is not his but hers.

The lioness has perfected insatiability. In the course of several days of heat she will be ready again about every twenty minutes. We may grant that the male has risen heroically to the challenge, but heroism has been conducted within the confines of reason. If you discover two, even three great males in a lion pride—all getting along with an amiable lack of envy or jealousy—it is because it takes that many lions to handle one lioness.

Sexual insatiability—which I shall return to with the primate—was the first true advance in the natural history of sex since the invention of the penis, and it has not been entirely lost in the course of our evolution. Whatever the bragging of males—stags, bulls, or other types—it was a female idea. Whatever its worth, however, insatiability failed to turn the animal world over to an interminable orgy. There remained the limitation of heat or season or rut. Sex was an entertainment that could happen only just so often. Mammalian orders, through time, divided and subdivided, and varying possibilities came about. Some female rodents, with their quickly gestating, quickly maturing young, might come into season eight or ten times a year. At the other extreme was the elephant; four and a half years between seasons offers minimum opportunity for orgies. If I speak with compassion for the sexual life of the animal, and with intolerance for those fellow human beings who find something bestial about sex, then it is this rare animal carnival that I have in mind. Animals need their instincts. Lacking them, they might otherwise forget between seasons just how to go about it.

So matters stood. They went no further throughout the

general range of mammalian orders. In a few eccentric species—the lion, for example, or the equatorial antelope, the Uganda kob—the female comes into heat whenever she finishes lactating and completes her maternal chore. All around the year in such species there is limited opportunity. But for almost all—the seal or the walrus, the weasel or wolf, the shy roe deer or the tempestuous rhino—sex still consists of a brief seasonal devotion to bellowing and bristling. For the rest of the year you may put it out of your mind. In only one order, our own family of primates, did anything new come about. You may trace the advances of primate sexuality in direct correlation with the advances in primate intelligence. The first invention—on the part of the female, as one might expect—was something called *estrus*.

If we go all the way back to the prosimian—the pre-monkey of forty or fifty million years ago—we find sex proceeding in quite normal mammalian fashion. The true lemurs of Madagascar offer our best surviving example, and while present species may have evolved on the island, they so closely resemble anatomically their ancestors of the forgotten Eocene that there is little reason to believe they differ physiologically. Beautiful though they are, they suffer the misfortune of being quite stupid. In Zurich the world's greatest zoo-master, Heini Hediger, had a group of ring-tailed lemurs for many years. He could proceed through the crowded zoo and a monkey would spot him a hundred feet away and raise a cheerful commotion. But the lemurs in all that time never learned to distinguish him from other passing faces.

So it was that fifty million years ago lemurs thrived, but when monkeys came along the competition was too much. The lemur became extinct. Only on Madagascar, which became separated from the African mainland—or the Indian, we are not sure—so early that monkeys never reached it, have true lemurs survived. There you will find them—foxy-faced, high-haunched, leaping like grasshoppers. You might not recognize them as primates except for the tell-tale hands with fingernails, not claws and, contrary to myth, opposable thumbs. The fingers have little flexibility, it is true, but as you compare the lemur's hand with your own, you will have a memorable sensation of looking at yourself in some antique mirror.

The lemur, like the deepest point of perspective in a painting, presents us with our deepest point of penetration in the story of primate sexuality. Until the astonishing adventures of the evolving human being, it is a straightforward story of the female role in species that have an expanding brain. The lemur mother was as free of problems as she was free of intelligence. Nicely programmed with instincts, her infant, born with a clinging reflex, latched on to its mother's belly. For about three months she suffered not even the maternal experience of a stomach ache, and she leaped through the trees as the equal of any unencumbered male. Then for a short few months the infant immobilized her with its need for care. But by six months or so it was independent, and so again was she. Notable was the sexual equality in lemur bands. She, just as likely as he, might be the leader. It never happened again in primate history.

The brain was the problem or the opportunity, depending how one wishes to regard it. Lemur young had so little to learn that the mother had little to give. Instincts flourished, the young were on their own, and so was she. The female retained the mammal generality and the sexual season. Whatever the joys of sex, they came once a year. The beautiful ring-tail of southeastern Madagascar, a primate species quite unique in that females may actually be dominant over males, has things arranged so that all females come into sexual season simultaneously. I am not sure that this is a good idea from the male's point of view (or even from that of society) since, with a savagery also unique among primates, they

79

must fight each other for pleasure's brief access. Nor am I sure that female ascendancy was worth the price of asexuality fifty weeks a year. It is a question I leave to the debate of others.

Whatever the advantages or the disadvantages of the lemur's moronic life, they were not to last. Right down the middle of the primate mainstream came the brainy Old World monkey, and the lemur was finished. With the monkey came not only the expanding brain, but decreasing dependence on instinct, increasing dependence on the lessons of experience, far slower maturing of offspring while they learned the tricks of monkey life, consequent immobilization of the monkey mother by her exasperating dependents, a consequent dependence on the whole society by the vulnerable mother and her heedless offspring, and a deplorable enhancement of male dominance in a society that neither mother nor young could survive without.

A sad story, perhaps, from the female view. Once in a while you came on a monkey species, like the savannah baboon, in which a few big males assumed at least the responsibility of protection. Or the South American marmoset, in which the father seemed pleased to carry the babies about. Or that remarkable development in the Japanese monkey, which seems to be cultural. Of ten long-observed troops superbly recorded by Japanese scientists, there are three in which not fathers but alpha males have lent a helping hand. The female frequently brings into the world a new infant before the previous one is equal to it. Then the male leaders of the troops—and only these alphas—step in to become surrogate mothers, patient and gentle. Since the character trait is not general in the species, it must seem one of fashion, a means of demonstrating one's high status as, in another species, satisfaction might be gained by the purchase of a Rolls-Royce. Yet one must wonder.

There are bisexual propensities in the animal that Sigmund Freud had never heard about when he pondered bisexuality in the human being. A long-held folk tale in Hungary was that of the drunken cock. If a peasant had problems with weasels, for example, that a brooding hen could not handle, then the idea was to take a rooster, souse him with slivovitz, and put him on the nest with the chicks. He'd handle things. It seemed one of those myths, like Adam and Eve.

Then, a very few years ago, scientists of weird bent decided to try it out in an experimental situation. They set up the hen, the chicks, the potential predator. They selected a belligerent rooster. If there was a weakness in the experiment, it was probably that they had no slivovitz handy and resorted to something as commonplace as whisky. But they produced a drunken cock. Lo, he behaved precisely according to peasant understanding. Placed on the nest, he clucked just as the hen would do, and the chicks responded with their comforted chirps. When confronted with a stuffed weasel, however, he responded as only a cock of the walk would—he attacked. The Hungarians were right.

There is no real answer. The chicken is a domesticated animal, and so probably is a mixed-up being. Japanese monkeys have an unbelievable capacity for cultural assimilation, so they don't count. New World monkeys have even developed that fifth arm, the prehensile tail, of such immense selective advantage for a life in the trees that one cannot understand why Old World monkeys did not develop one too. But it did not happen. The apes, large and small, even lost their tails completely. In evolutionary biology one must never get too lost in the logic of selective advantage.

What happened was what happened. And in the Old World mainstream—the only primate course that would lead to human existence—monkey mothers had to settle for being mothers. Whatever her nostalgia for the lemur's egalitarian, emancipated life, the female had to accept her role as a kind of prison warden, jailed as much as her troublesome off-spring by the infant's slow-growing brain. Variety is a character of primate social life. In a few species like the gibbon and the South American callicebus, male and female might pair, so that she at least has company. In a few, as I have noted, the male might lend a helping hand. In a polygamous species like the patas, the male overlord might act as protector, just as an unchallengeable oligarchy acts as a police force in the large mixed troops of the common baboon. But the policemen share no domestic burdens, and even protection is rare. If the male has remained within the primate society, his contribution to child-raising, made with minimum effort, has been largely educational. Through imitation the juveniles come slowly to know the ways of adult life. Yet his example has been less than elevating, since normally he has preferred the companionship of other males; pub-crawlers all, they have ignored the female, ignored the young, pursued their own pleasures.

They left everything to her. And so regularly she produced her new infant, nourished it, protected it. Regularly the tropical sun came up, the tropical sun went down. Regularly the tropical seasons of rain and dry provided the rhythm of life and obligation; just as regularly the millions of years went by. Somewhere along the way she made the primate invention of estrus. And while I should never claim that boredom entered into the evolutionary formula, still estrus did much to enliven monkey life, and to bring to the female a degree of attention that no primate had ever enjoyed before.

Estrus—in the monkey and the ape as well—is that period of sexual receptivity in the female that comes not once every interminable year but as frequently as every lunar month. Nothing like it in the primate line had ever happened before. Estrus was the sexual jackpot. Just to make things more interesting, the primate female combined it with insatiability; and in most species with a remarkably measured promiscuity. One female, in a period of estrus lasting perhaps five days, could provide fun for all and at the same time secure for herself a maximum of male attention.

I have noted that the sexual appetite of the lioness has induced in the lion—or perhaps enforced on him—a most amiable lack of jealousy concerning fellows of his own pride. The same happy state of emotional affairs came about in the normal current of ape and monkey life. As always there are exceptions such as the polygamous species of the arid northern regions of Uganda, Ethiopia, and the Sudan. Here you find the harem social-pattern, with a single jealous male guarding his female property. Behavior so impractical would puzzle a chimp, who tends to take life as he finds it. I do not believe that in all of Goodall's long study of her group of chimpanzees above Lake Tanganyika she ever observed a serious sexual conflict between males. And if jealousy existed in the repertory of chimp behavior, then most surely it was the surpassing sex-appeal of an old female named Flo who would have occasioned it.

For the whole story of Flo, one must read Goodall's book. Here was an old, ugly, battered creature whose appeal for males Goodall first put down to an experienced life. Yet this did not explain it, as she later discovered. Some females might come into estrus and go virtually ignored. Another old female, nervous at all seasons around males, lighted no fires; perhaps that had something to do with it, since Flo was always at ease with the fellows. There was something more, however, for she was as superb a mother as the forest could provide. Perhaps in this she was exceptional. But no matter what their age, her offspring seemed never to lose their affection for her. Just as in the human being one encounters those immense individual differences of personal endowment which psychologists so frequently ignore, so Flo must simply be accepted as a character. And when Flo came into estrus, how the word went around. On their first awed exposure to

Flo's generous affections, Goodall and van Lawick watched their ageing character—with her teeth worn down to the gums, her thinning, fading hair, her skinny, sagging frame—surrounded by nine adult males each cheerfully waiting his turn, and receiving it.

While courtship, pairing, mutual grooming, geographical confinement to a territory, and sometimes mutual concern for the young may all have contributed bonds to a social life, still from its earliest beginnings the sex act itself had never amounted to anything more—with one qualification—than the simplest and most economical means of getting a female in reproductive condition. Through the physiology and the enthusiasm of the primate female, sex entered that new region, entertainment. But there remained the qualification. Through one means or another natural selection, accepting a significantly superior genetic potential in some males, had always sorted about for those most qualified to leave their genes to the succeeding generation. Through the device of territory, the competition for exclusive bits of real estate among males was matched in the female by sexual unresponsiveness to any but the landed gentry. Through the device of dominance in a species living in social groups, only those males reaching the highest rungs of the social hierarchy might receive the sexual franchise. Through the device of psychological castration, those males who failed to gain the franchise of territory or status lost sexual motivation and became, to use the ornithologist's term, unemployed.

And so one must reflect: praiseworthy though this stunning primate sexual breakthrough may have been, introducing a regime of utmost democracy with satisfaction and fun for all, what happened to natural selection? How could the evolutionary process have tolerated the abandonment of its central dynamic? In such a roundabout of pleasures, there seems no pattern at all to determine the union of sperm and ovum as anything but random. Why did not apes and monkeys become extinct as a reward for their hedon-istic departure? Well, one must pause again, but this time with reverence. It was the female who solved that one, too.

Most primate species have retained a certain deference for the old-time mammalian annual season in that there are times of year in which, for all the estrus and the copula-tion, pregnancy does not come about. In such species births are rare except within a few months. It is like a natural form of birth control, and—as I described at length in *The Social Contract*—such restraints, though we may not quite understand them, are common in animal populations. The process may answer the question of why there are not too many monkeys, but it does not solve the problem of selection when pregnancy does come about. The primate female an-swered this one through the combination of an astonishing physiological innovation with plain, old-fashioned snobbish-ness.

There does not exist a truly egalitarian primate society. The same might be said of all societies of vertebrate animals, with a certain reservation for such massive groups as the herring school, in which the individual vanishes in over-whelming mediocre seas. But wherever members of a group are recognized as individuals, we will find some pattern of competition and dominance. In the summer of 1973 my wife and I with Konrad Lorenz, at the Max Planck Institute's Bavarian goose pond where he then lived and worked, watched a record-breaking fight between two fourteen-day-old goslings, each out to establish his dominance. One could not believe that such adorable, fluffy, fragile little creatures (neither of whom, I firmly suspect, could have learned any-thing from television) could fight for so long. Yet that is how it goes from a most early age, and orders of dominance once established mean that later on there will be very little fight-ing. It is one of the most significant yet least understood prin-

85

ciples that the Nobel prizewinner has contributed to our new knowledge of nature.

Among primate societies establishment of dominance is universal and may result not only in male hierarchies but, as in the Japanese monkey, female hierarchies as well. The sorting process may come about through very little fighting, simply through quick acceptance by the subordinate as to who is entitled to be listed in the animal Who's Who. The consequent hierarchy may be ruthlessly despotic, as in the savannah baboon, or equally despotic but benevolent, as in the gorilla. Our egalitarian dreams demanded that the chimpanzee be innocent of such status-seeking aggressions, and so such an early study as that of the Reynolds confirmed not so much the ways of the chimp as the utopian dreams of men. Then came Goodall's ten-year study, and an end to many a fantasy about the chimp. The male chimp is not only as aggressive concerning his status as any primate we know but, perhaps because he is brighter, does not necessarily accept the decisions of youth; he is capable of revolution at any stage of his adult career. And he is capable likewise of terrorizing the subordinate female whenever the mood comes upon him. Our genial cousin, as it turns out, demonstrates all too many a human trait.

In any society of monkeys and apes, what the female faced was this: a hierarchy of males that might most gently be described as an arrangement in which some had greater influence on the social direction than did others. She faced likewise the situation that never since the lamented lemur had there been a primate species in which males were not dominant over females, just as adults were not dominant over young. So, with these new possibilities of estrus, she combined sexual generosity with some excellent social improvements.

India's rhesus monkey, since the early observations of C. R. Carpenter beginning in the 1930's, has been the most widely observed of all primates. The rhesus has a strict order of dominance, from a single male with signaled upraised tail, down to Number Last, the omega. When the female comes into estrus, she will take on anybody, but the alpha will ignore her. So as her sexual heat intensifies, she moves up the social ladder. Her desirability eliminates those fervid adolescents, who first had their fun, in favor of the rhesus bourgeoisie, who now have their entertainment. No female snobbishness rejects the rhesus middle class, but there comes a time when she will form a consort relationship with Number 1 or Number 2, whatever is the best she can manage. Only then does her egg descend from the ovary, to be fertilized by an alpha male.

I do not believe that physiologically this conclusion has been investigated in sufficient primate species to be regarded as primate truth. Neither do I believe that many primate students will dispute its present high probability. A quite staggering combination of physiological directives has been combined with a behavioral directive to preserve natural selection. You *can* have your cake and eat it; the primate female proved it.

We have been bombarded in the twentieth century with the doomsday attitude. It has varied little from the turn-of-the-century Freudian interpretation that if we dreamed of a gun we were in truth handling the penis. (I myself would quite reverse the symbolism.) Sex was all, and if you had problems in the office, it was because you had problems in bed. (Again I would reverse the symbolism.) So, in Freudian terms, when a man went to bed with a woman, empires rose or empires fell. I do not accept it.

Neither do I accept the present technological approach in which sexual partners go to bed each with their glasses on, the more carefully to read the latest sex manual with numbered instructions as to what to do next. It is all far too much in accord with our present reverence for the assembly line, automation, and computerized life. The technologists have replaced the timidities of ignorance with the nightmares of incompetence.

Thankfully I recall that in my first evolutionary book I

described sex as "the entertainment instinct." That is what the primate female introduced to our animal legacy: the proposition that sex is fun. And that is what the human female elaborated, long ages ago I believe, far beyond the rollicking imaginations of chimp or rhesus monkey or savannah baboon.

When we came out of the forests for good and all, when we lost our climbing feet and could never go back, when we faced the vast yellow immensity of the African savannah and had to discover new strongholds of cooperation to replace the old strongholds of the trees, then what had been a social preference in monkey or ape became a social imperative for the new kind of being.

Until a decade or so ago, when the first wave of primate studies came along, there had been a tendency in the sciences to accept an old dictum that primate sociality was a consequence of primate sexuality. Males and females embraced a mixed social life, better to enjoy the opportunities of sex. With our expanding knowledge of the primate in the wild, the dictum became rapidly obsolete. A contrary truth became evident: primate sexuality was the consequence, not the cause, of primate social life. Basic to that life was the handicap of slow-growing young, the long years of learning, and the immobilization and vulnerability of mothers. Without the group, few would be the young who lived to maturity. Yet since basic food was never shared, concerted primate defense was rare, and a scramble up a tree remained the normal response to emergencies, one cannot say that social life was a daily do-or-die proposition.

All changed once the earth beneath us became the only home we should ever know, just as all changed when our daily fruit became our daily meat and our daily bread remained many millions of years in the future. We retained all the ape disadvantages of slow-growing young and the vulnerable mother. But we accepted new hazards: the danger of predators whom we once could all but ignore with our arboreal security; the changes of seasons, and the unpredictability of the weather from year to year, meaningless in the eternal forest; the changing ways of game animals with the deprivations or generosities of seasons; above all, the sharing of food, which meant for the mother a day-to-day dependence on male competence.

Perhaps there are those among us whose intuitions exceed their education and who emotionally reject the hunting hypothesis for the quite sound conclusion that it meant dependence of the female on the male; just as there are those among us who prefer that portrait of humankind which pictures our earliest ancestors as a panorama of women and children gathering the essential fruits of the land while their men go off chasing animals. I find it difficult otherwise to comprehend why a modern, educated, sophisticated society should, like hay-fever victims in the presence of pollen, so sneeze at the idea of ancestral dependence on meat. The ancestral mother had too many survival problems to indulge in the psychosomatic ailments which we can afford today.

The mother, her young, and the next generation depended almost totally on the proficiency of the adult males of her society. When the males failed again and again at the hunt, the little band died of quite natural causes. We may think of such early times as one in which hundreds, even thousands of such bands in the vastness of Africa made the transition from forest to savannah life. Few left their fossilized bones for contemporary inspection. Mostly they just died and left their remains to oblivion, and, when it happened without offspring, to extinction.

There can be little doubt in my own mind that the female carried on the ape tradition of dedication to her young. What had to develop, though, was what I think of as a sexually bipolar society. It was not the society of the elephant, the mountain sheep, or that inconspicuous rodent, the yellow-bellied marmot, in which the male has one function: to show up at the right sexual moment, do his spermatic duty, and vanish; the female will take care of everything. Neither was it the society of the advancing primate in which the male was necessary—if not for protection, then at least for educational example, to inspire the learning young. In the meat-eating hominid the male was pragmatically necessary, or in a very few days everybody died from a diet of spinach.

And so, as I see it, a bipolar society came about with new challenges for integration. Unquestionably mothers and young foraged for whatever the plant world could provide. I joke about spinach, yet undoubtedly there were leafy greens, a few fruits in season, and honey, as I have described, that gave us needed vitamins and calories when seasons made them available. The chimp who eats meat takes a leaf or two now and then with startling resemblance to the American eating his inevitable steak with his inevitable salad. But in even our earliest nonreturn adventures into savannah life, there had to be a bipolar development of primate society. There had to be those who stayed more or less home, the guardians and the guarded who would provide us with a successor generation, and there had to be those who ventured, perhaps far, to gain us the protein without which we could not survive.

Sexual segregation within the society became the rule when we became dependent on meat-eating. I have given small space so far to the evolutionary development of the hunting band, because while its inheritance extends into our day, still in its evolutionary time the most immediate consequence was sexual. The hunting band was that assembly of adult males who went out on daily forays to secure meat. We think of it as all-male, though there was no necessary reason that childless females could not have joined it. There were reasons in plenty, however, that juveniles could not be a part. The band as a whole, taking concerted risks in its hunt, could not tolerate weak members. The deficiency of one could mean the annihilation of all. The hunting band, facing dangerous prey, presented us with our first test of natural selection on the savannah. Could we cooperate, or could we not?

Dominance, a revolutionary social necessity even in the carefree forest life, became a day-to-day survival institution in the lives of cooperating hunters. In any group of eight or ten, random chance would dictate that one at least had superior capacities. The survival value of social organization rests on the benefit that one superior individual confers even on the group's last member. Yet whatever his ingenuity, experience, judgment, or courage, it was meaningless without the willingness of others to risk and to follow. And while we admire the courage and cooperation of the baboon male oligarchy, still, male cooperation on a human scale was without primate precedent. We succeeded—enough of us—or there would be no human beings. The success was a long stride in the evolution of human uniqueness, one that could never have been taken by a vegetarian. But its success brought about a social dilemma that could never have occurred in the forest.

I have referred to the bipolar direction of our new, evolving society. Male monkeys or apes may prefer the company of their own sex, but no survival pressure rests on it. Now came a *functional* segregation of males. In the course of daily necessity, adult males went their way to form their own bonds of loyalty and group risk. The adult female constrained by her offspring could not join them. She had no choice but to remain in a localized area—the rudimentary home—from which she and her maturing young could make forays to snare an ancestral rabbit, snatch a tortoise, gather swarming edible insects, dig up the rare edible root, or collect the seasonal berries and nuts. Her range was as limited as the demands of her newest infant.

And so came about this sexual segregation in the daily life; the males to their hunting range, the females and young

91

to their homesite. (We think of it today as the office and the home.) Her collections of food were undoubtedly important in terms of vitamins, but it was low-calorie. The survival of the reproductive group depended on the return of the males with whatever bacon they had managed.

In any speculative reconstruction of the human past, one must keep in mind not only the enormous innovation of male cooperation in the hunt, but the psychological abyss that exists between the implacable selfishness of the earlier primate male, and the responsibility of our own male line. They did not hunt for immediate gratification. They hunted for the nourishment of their females and their young. And while it is all very well to presume that they *knew* that they would have no inheritors if they did not bring the meat back home, still, such a concept would give any biologist the shudders, and I am a Darwinian. The sudden access of altruism smacks of divine intervention. It is true that there is many a generous bird species in which paternal responsibility commands fields of sacrifice. It is also true that as certain species of gulls will bring home their gleanings to regurgitate into the mouths of their young, certain natural predators like the African hunting dog will do quite the same. Still, these are unrelated species, and there is nothing in our family tree—from tarsier to lemur to monkey to ape—to indicate that paternal responsibility could go this far. Nor is there any reason to believe that we, with our ape brain encountering the challenges of the hunting life, had any impressive advantages over our ancestors in terms of *knowing* what the next generation would demand. We show little enough such propensity today.

I accept the view of many biologists that female invention of year-round sexual responsiveness was the biological answer to the problem of a bipolar society. When Goodall's Flo came into spectacular estrus and for a week was followed about by her male retinue, then took a rest for a few days, then came back spectacularly into further sexual attention for two or three weeks, it was the last to be heard of Flo, sexually, for a good five years. I cannot believe that such chimpanzee comings-and-goings were good enough for the evolving, dependent human female. So came about a physiological sexual revolution, like so many others in our history without precedent.

And a revolution it was. Year-round sexual receptivity on the part of the human female was perhaps the most astonishing innovation that had ever come about since the biological introduction of sex itself, a half-billion years ago or more. And the female did it. Am I to believe that the innovation had no relation to the commands of a bipolar society in which the men had to bring the meat back home? I should be derogating the female if I were to assume a statistical improbability, that it was all coincidence.

In Darwinian terms, every selective advantage rested on the reproductive success of a social group so sexually segregated. Certain groups survived and gave to us their seed, not just forgotten fossils. The male in time might become habituated to his role as the provider, but I believe, though it is difficult to prove, that the lure of year-round female sexual attraction kept the previously careless male on his necessary rounds.

What we do not know about these early eons of sexual revolution will absorb decades of future research. I believe that most authorities will agree that with bipedal stature came the beginnings of frontal copulation. Such a sexual possibility was not truly denied the ape, though the inquisitive chimpanzee seems to have held firmly to lizard-lion tradition. George Schaller's investigation of the mountain gorilla has revealed an occasional exploration. But gorilla adventure is so low-sexed in comparison with the chimpanzee that one has little to go upon. Against such a background, a mere anecdotal experience becomes of a certain importance. Face-to-face sex-

93

ual intercourse was to become, I believe, an important development in the course of the human sexual adventure.

In Uganda, within a mile or so of the Congo border, there was in its time a hotel of nine beds, with kerosene light, catering almost entirely to a clientele of scientists and dedicated tourists who cared about gorillas. On the slopes of the volcano, Mount Muhavura, that loomed above us, were diminishing numbers of gorillas who lived off the shoots of a bamboo forest that thrived at about ten or eleven thousand feet in altitude. And there was a guide—half Watusi, tall and lean-shanked after the manner of his people—who for twenty years had indefatigably climbed the volcano to watch gorilla goings-on. His name was Reuben. Since he did not possess a doctor's degree, his name, Reuben, is all that we can record. Yet his voice was authentic and so was accepted by all those who in those days visited the volcano. So when the hotel's proprietor, Walter Baumgartel, told me one day that Reuben had witnessed frontal copulation between gorillas, I was naturally curious. We got hold of Reuben.

He was unexpectedly shy about the matter. Baumgartel reassured him that I was a doctor (which of course I was not) and so everything was all right. So Reuben reluctantly lay down on the verandah floor to reenact the scene he had once witnessed. Assuming the female's position, he spread his long shanks and started moaning. At this point my wife entered. Reuben lost his hat. Again Baumgartel tried to reassure him: "It's all right, she's a doctor too." But by then Reuben had retrieved his hat and was well down the road towards his house.

That was the closest I ever came to frontal copulation in the ape. Such a rare observation as Reuben's—once in twenty years of almost daily gorilla observation—demonstrated merely that it could happen. The lizard-lion approach, fashionable for two hundred million years, held on. And for all we know, conservatism being what it is, the opportunities of erect posture may have brought about no revolutions for a very long time. But change had to come, since any sexual improvement enhanced the solidarity of our bipolar society. And frontal copulation individualized and intensified the sexual relationship.

One must be most cautious about speculation in areas such as permanent sexual arrangements, for which we have no evidence at all. Pairing and lifelong monogamy have examples through the animal world, from the Arctic skua to the gibbon, from the albatross perhaps even to the wolf. Yet while monogamy may occur, it is rare in primates and social predators, in which promiscuity seems a more general rule. Nevertheless, polygamy has its adherents, such as the permanent harem dominated by a single male that one finds in the patas monkey, the hamadryas baboon, and the gelada, or in the lion pride dominated by one or more males. There is as wide an assortment of mating arrangements in the animal world as there are marriage customs in the human world. Robin Fox has made the cynical observation that anthropology's preoccupation with varying marriage customs ignores the arrangement that all peoples have in common: adultery.

What is misleading is the great ape example of total promiscuity. We are discovering how in many ways our terrestrial hunting life led us into necessary innovation. Ruled out is the harem possibility, since one hunter could never have supported more than one woman and her offspring. The ratio of adult males to adult females must have been close to 1 to 1. But this does not guarantee monogamy. Our hunting was communal, our life at the home-site may have been communal as well. A powerful attachment on the part of the male provider for his wife and children might seem a motive of selective value. But we must keep in mind the almost total unlikelihood that until fairly recent times any association existed between the sexual act and the bearing of children. There are contemporary primitive peoples, like the Trobri-

95

anders and certain Australian aborigines, to whom the idea never occurred. And it is remarkable how in the souvenirs of Cro-Magnon man—ourselves—female fertility figures abound, whereas phallic symbols are rare.

Evidence and speculative considerations are so contradictory that, while they may be persuasive to others, I myself have no answer to the origins of monogamy. An argument favoring it is that frontal copulation lent strong encouragement to individual attachment. The missionary position may presently be derogated by our fashionable sexual technicians, but at least you knew who you were doing it with; and if the relation was agreeable, someday we might call it love. One consequence must be fairly sure: the shift of sexual focus from rear to front, whatever marital rearrangements resulted, brought on some remarkable anatomical rearrangements.

I agree entirely with my friend, Desmond Morris, that there can be no possible explanation for the enlargement of the female breast except as a sexual releaser. Gone were the days of the swollen pink bottom, or of the bull giraffe's sampling the female's urine to find out how she is coming along. Gone likewise were the days when the female teat carried no sexual attraction whatsoever. Frontal sexual approaches demanded frontal enticements, and so the breasts enlarged along with the exaggerated pigmentation of the aureole. I recognize, just as Morris discovered, that the idea offends many traditionalists, who must associate the breast with the suckling babe. Yet the great ape has no difficulty at all feeding her infant from what is little more than a faucet, and had the enlargement of breasts not been of sexual advantage, I find it difficult to believe that they would have evolved at all. As impediments to a woman's activity, they are maladaptive.

But breasts were not the only rearrangement of the sexual furniture brought about by frontal negotiations. The mouth and the eyes took on new significance. In one of his most amusing studies Oxford's Niko Tinbergen—along with Lorenz a Nobel prizewinner—experimented with what he termed "supernormal stimuli." Giant dummy eggs six times natural size were introduced in the incubating season to a sea bird called the oyster-catcher. She went crazy in her frantic efforts to cover it. No normal egg ever excited her like these great dummies. With exquisite restraint Tinbergen commented that perhaps now we can understand lipstick.

The importance of the mouth (and why females do not have beards) is best examined through subjective recollection, since, despite Tinbergen's urging, the examination of "supernormal stimuli" has been neglected by the sciences. We tend in our time, as I have so frequently commented, to ascribe all such responses to cultural influence. But when it comes to eyes, the research of Eckhard Hess, the remarkable professor of psychology at the University of Chicago, has presented behaviorist psychology with a problem so far beyond explanation that the pseudoscience has taken its normal course of ignoring it.

Admittedly Hess's discovery has come as just another wild adventure in the scientific explosion of the past decade. It has had to compete with continental drift, plate tectonics, geomagnetic reversals, ever-new discoveries of the first man, people walking on the moon, and disillusionment with highrise housing. The competition has been tough. If I expand on his discovery here, it is not only to compensate for the little public attention it has aroused, or because I regard it as of large significance, but also because it tells a portion of the story that I am telling, the radical innovations that have come about in the evolution of human sexuality.

The discovery was quite simply this: that the pupils of one's eyes—yours or mine—expand or contract not entirely in accord with the level of illumination, but in direct correlation with our interest in the object or the subject before us. Very early in his research he found an odd conclusion. This

97

was in 1964, when that most right-wing of possible candidates, Barry Goldwater, was running for president. At a liberal university like Chicago, Goldwater's name was a very bad word. Yet Hess found that among student volunteers for his experiments, confronted by a long series of photographs of celebrities, about one-third demonstrated expansion of their pupils when confronted with Goldwater. So he tried art. At Chicago, avant-garde in all things, nonobjective art was what one had to adore. Yet a good third of his subjects, confronted by a Pollock or a Rothko, demonstrated pupil contraction. (He had devised an elaborate way of making film of the response, just to keep things scientific.) What he was discovering, of course, was that an involuntary mechanism, regulating through expansion or contraction of the eye's pupil, told the truth about human response that the mind's rationalizations could not deny.

With good reason Eckhard Hess calls his astonishing new book *The Tell-Tale Eye*. His research took him far from a Chicago laboratory into peculiar by-streets of custom. Chinese jade-dealers, for example, habitually watch their customer's eyes for clues as to how much to ask. Turkish rug-buyers have found it to their interest to wear dark glasses. Not all has been a matter of American political campaigns or fashions in art. So Hess turned his experiments to unconscious reflexes of males and females. He found that a woman's pupils will dilate when she comes on the photograph of a baby, the male's not at all. He found that in a series of random photographs, that of a nude woman will have no response in the female pupil, plenty in the male; predictably enough, the photograph of a nude male will have the opposite responses. Such unconscious biological reflexes must make unpleasant reading for those who believe that sex roles are learned.

Yet much in human relations becomes suddenly explicable. When a woman meets a man who actively interests her sexually, the pupils of her eyes expand. (It is a typical Lorenzian sexual releaser.) And he—how many times in our literaure have we recorded the general idea, "There was something in her eyes"—responds to her signal with his own dilations. It is a basic finding of ethology that the female animal usually provides the signal to release the male urge. What is remarkable is that we have obeyed the signal without for a moment understanding it. Courtesans may have had a clue, since for centuries they used belladonna to expand their eyes' pupils. Less professional females had no need for belladonna.

All came naturally. The female gives her involuntary signal. The male, looking into her eyes, says to himself for reasons quite obscure to him that this woman is ready, and proceeds according to normal male ways. Yet how amazing it is that the communication was so innate that we never knew, until Hess, of its existence. Still more amazing, how long the frontal approaches of the sexes must have been in human vogue to produce through natural selection a frontal biological signal so subtle.

Well, I don't know how long. But there was another anatomical change of presumably older order that came about with frontal copulation. It has to do with hair, or fur. And here I must disagree most abruptly with Desmond Morris, who should have known better. He attributed the nakedness of his ape to the problem of a predator's coursing equatorial savannahs, and overheating. Yet why didn't the cheetah, the leopard, the hyena, the enigmatic hunting dog, expending far more energy than did we with our limited feet, not lose theirs? But more important: why was it that the female, who can't have done much hunting, has lost her fur so much more incisively than the male?

As you cast your mind about through our descendant peoples, a remarkable variation in hairlessness becomes evident. Concerning males, between the beardless American Indian and the hairy Swede there is a considerable gap. But there is no gap among females. In our species the female has

99

universally become hairless except in certain quite localized regions. I dislike intensely departing from the conclusions of my colleague Desmond Morris, but the nakedness of the human ape could not have been the consequence of the hunting life. It was a necessary consequence of sexual display on the part of the human female. Her frontal sexual enticements became openly displayed. No chest hair obscured her breasts, no beard the enticements of her mouth, no forward-growing head-hair, as in the sheepdog, her eyes.

So female invention went on. And the latest—though I should never consider the last—was the female orgasm. The capacity varies so widely among individuals that one must suspect a very recent evolutionary heritage. The male's capacity, two hundred million years old, is automatic. The female's, varying so remarkably, one must suspect is fairly new in evolutionary terms and so is subject to the inhibitions of culture. But this we may suspect:

The female orgasm through enhancement of female desire provided one further guarantee that the males would return from the hunt. The male might be tired; female desire would refresh him. The male's orgasm, perfected through the ages, is a reflex; the female's demands a certain discipline, a concentration on the part of the central nervous system. I should doubt very much that female reward preceded by long the enlargement of the great human brain.

The female orgasm was the last—at least until now—of that long line of female inventions contributing to human sexual uniqueness, and at the same time—quite in accord with Darwinian thought—advancing the probability that her young would survive. The dedicated biologist may object to my use of the term *inventions,* and of course he is right. The orgasm was no more a conscious invention than was the expansion of the pupil of the eye, concerning which we have had no consciousness at all. But I cannot forever be reciting the formula of variation, natural selection, and survival value.

That today you and I through cultural intervention are protected from further biological evolution is a fallacy of utmost myopia. The very history of our sexual adventure must give us thought: every turn has been dictated by an advancing necessity for social solidarity, and for the tie of the fathers to their young. In a time of cultural disintegration of families and societies, are we to believe that the cultural animal now enjoys some magic protection from biological consequences, perhaps of a most unhappy order?

Whatever may happen, the female, at least in the past, has done her heroic best to preserve a new kind of being in a new kind of world.

Territory Revisited

Slowly, ever so slowly, we began to assemble those qualities anatomical and behavioral that we regard as distinctively human. They did not all come about one at a time. We did not develop a capacity for leadership and concerted action among males while at the same time deferring such problems as the solidarity of the whole social group, the sharing of food, and male responsibility till some future time. All came as immediate necessities without which we could not survive as primate hunters. Neither did what we regard as humanity wait for the ordered measures of a pharaoh's palace or a background of mumbling priests, just as it did not wait for profound discussions on the philosopher's walk, or even for the big brain that would make such discussions an event of future significance. Humanity evolved beneath the canopy of African skies on the immense card table of the African savannah. We took a mutational gamble on this quality or that; we left descendants or we did not; we won or we lost.

We must not be misled into believing that the evolutionary assembly of the human being took place along any straight line. I think that what we must visualize, in the time of the forests' slow withdrawal, was the launching on the yellow seas of terrestrial commitment of many a descendant of the forest ape, to float or to sink. These were local populations. What was happening was an ecological adventure. Who could best survive a quite new environmental challenge? A single environmental problem, that of existing without the stronghold of the trees on a diet basically of meat, with a single endowment of various ape assets and liabilities, meant a certain parallel or convergent evolution. The foot *had* to develop a terrestrial accommodation, or in extinction you could forget the whole adventure. So whatever our origins there was a single selective pressure to develop the singular qualities that we regard as human.

A puzzler these days is the sudden accumulation of fossil human relics from about three million years ago. In the time when I was preparing *African Genesis,* and we had only the South African discoveries as evidence, we saw our ancestral family of australopithecines divided quite neatly between two species: *africanus,* which Raymond Dart had discovered, and *robustus,* which Robert Broom discovered, a heavyweight who even boasted a skull-crest comparable to that of the gorilla. The conclusion was obvious that the lithe, small, evidently carnivorous *africanus* was the one who came closest to the human line. John Robinson, Broom's heir, and an authority whom I respect, once described *robustus* to me as "the dumb cousin." The description will do. It was about then, as I have recorded early in this narrative, that I decided that we should find the final answers in East Africa, two thousand miles to the north, not in the suburbs of Johannesburg.

Not answers, but proliferating problems have been pouring in for the last five years from East Africa. It was our evolutionary metropolis with little doubt. Nevertheless, like the ethnic groups one finds in Manhattan, these early beings existed in startling variety. *Africanus* is there, and the dumb cousin, but there were others that in our South African days of speculative innocence we could not anticipate. All, in my opinion—though this is controversial—fall within the range of australopithecine definition: a being resembling ourselves in dentition and erect posture, but with a brain-size nearer to the ape's. Most startling has been Richard Leakey's widely publicized discovery of "East Rudolf man," a being at least a foot taller than *africanus* and with a brain which, while only about half the size of our own, was still larger than that of any other known australopithecine. Properly, perhaps, he has claimed that his discovery had crossed the human threshold, and so refers to it as *Homo*. Improperly, I believe, he has denied its australopithecine heritage. If we are to accept the human line of evolutionary origin—I suggested this in my first chapter—as independent of other small-brained hominids, we are right back to special creation, if not to divine intervention. And the question, Why is man man?, can be referred to the department of neometaphysics.

Richard Leakcy's discovery consists of several valid fossils with valid dates almost three million years old. Problems concerning East Rudolf man's ancestors are exceeded, I believe, by problems concerning his descendants. Here he was, living in a fairly limited area that includes the Omo river valley just to the north of Lake Rudolf with a variety of hominid beings who have contributed in these recent years the remains of about two hundred individuals. So superior was he in stature, presumably in strength, and definitely in brain-size, that in terms of natural selection the observer is tempted to conclude that he alone would have dominated our succeeding evolutionary history. He doesn't; not only that, he vanishes. Not until a few hundred thousand years ago, with *Homo erectus* (Pekin man, Java man, Heidelberg man and fossils from Algeria, South Africa, and Hungary) do we come on a comparable being. Can the fossil record be that incomplete? Well, if the discoveries of the last few years are to be projected into the future, then we may have some more shocks and surprises. Nevertheless, Richard Leakey's parents, in a lifetime of research in East Africa's Olduvai Gorge, came up with about forty hominid remains between one and two million years old. None is as advanced as East Rudolf man. Perhaps his giant qualities were lost in hybridization with such small hominids as Johanson is finding in Ethiopia. But if he was the first man, then what happened to the second?

Such are the complications and confusions that must afflict the anthropologist, field or armchair, in the midst of a time of discovery. Sooner or later we shall undoubtedly sort out our semantics. But for a very long time we must struggle with an African anthropology that from its inception has reflected a scene not only of evolving human beings but of evolving human egos. The development in a field so new is both normal and desirable. Any natural selection of ideas could have operated only if the original proponents had with stubborn egotism refused to bow to conventional assumptions. So it was with Dart, with Broom, with Louis Leakey. A new generation of anthropological Vasco da Gamas comes along, and if they do not as stubbornly defend their so often mutually exclusive opinions, then we shall all be the losers in our struggle to gain a greater understanding of our nature.

So I offer here a suggestion that may well gain greater support from geneticists than from physical anthropologists, a suggestion which falls properly into a chapter titled *Territory Revisited*. The paleontologist has been frequently criticized, and with justification: behavior leaves no fossils. And as we probe about amongst the mysteries of the evolving human being three million years ago, and rummage through the human rubbish that time has left behind, we must never forget that anatomy fails to tell all. Extinction tells much. Something failed. But what if anatomically an ancient species had everything going for it—yet failed?

One hundred thousand years ago Neanderthal man dominated the human scene. It was the Ice Age. He had a brain larger on the average than our own. He was powerful, he was a superb hunter. Yet when Cro-Magnon—broadly speaking, modern man, ourselves—entered Europe 35,000 years ago, Neanderthal became promptly extinct. I shall return to this. But why did Neanderthal go while we remained? The fossil record tells nothing, or little. Cro-Magnon's cultural advances were considerable, but not decisive. His slightly smaller brain may have been far better organized than his predecessor's. But if so, then this is why brain-size tells us much but not all, and superior capacities of survival lie not in the area of anatomy but behavior, so let us move over to ethology.

Behavior leaves no fossils, it is true. But we are faced with a three-million-year-old mystery to which anatomy presents most doubtful clues. Some of these lost beings survived to leave their genes to the human line; some did not. We have the right to speculate about qualities that do not appear in the quantitative record. What I find a remarkable clue is the date. It was precisely the time initiating a massive change in world climate.

Another area of broad scientific advance in the past decade has been our knowledge of ancient climates. Nuclear physics, while presenting us with the doom-laden bomb, as a minor side-product gave us our present techniques of absolute dating based on the regular decay of radiogenic elements. Paleobotany, a quite new science, made another contribution with its techniques of analyzing fossil pollen to determine the changes of ancient landscapes—tundra for example giving way to conifer forests, conifers to hardwoods. Then the geologists came along. Whereas fifteen years ago we had all accepted the classic estimate of a million years as the boundary between the enduring Pliocene and our present variable Pleistocene, now discovery after discovery showed glaciers moving downhill in Iceland, in New Zealand, in the California Sierras, about 2.5 million years ago. Deep-sea drilling, such as that which revealed the Mediterranean desert and the Gibraltar waterfall, demonstrated that enormous icebergs moving north from the spreading Antarctic ice cap, were melting and depositing definable Antarctic sands on the ocean bottom almost as far north as the Cape of Good Hope. When? Two and a half million years ago.

So a revolution came to our thinking. The memorable Ice Age which had first spread across Europe six or seven hundred thousand years ago had been simply the climax of that far longer period of inexplicable change that we call the Pleistocene. Few must have been the earth's landscapes—and conditions of life—left unaffected by changes of rainfall, temperature, ocean currents, and prevailing winds that the new regime brought about.

Evolving man had to meet the changes head-on. It may be no more than a coincidence that we seem to have developed the human body in the durable, conservative Pliocene, and the human brain in the fickle, changeful Pleistocene. It may likewise be no more than a coincidence that at the three-million-year horizon in our history, so characterized by the variety of human experiments, all quite shortly in evolutionary terms would face an increasing tempo of change in environmental challenge. We know how they varied anatomically. Had some received from their Pliocene inheritance more appropriate behavior patterns than others? I am thinking specifically of territoriality and the social mind.

We know next to nothing about our Pliocene experience except its end products, which are today becoming visible. We do not even know how long it lasted from the time that we committed ourselves to the savannah, renounced the forest and its fruits, accepted hunting and meat-eating as our necessary condition of life. Experiments may have come early, as Louis Leakey's Miocene ramapithecines, fifteen million years old, suggest. Or the final separation of ape and man may have come somewhat later. But a date even as late as eight million years ago leaves little evolutionary room for such complex adaptations as the human foot and consequent straight-limbed bipedal posture that we find at the three-million-year horizon. Our Pliocene experience lasted for a long time, and that is about all one can say at present.

There are some reasonable assumptions, however, beyond cooperation, sharing of food, the beginnings at least of sexual rearrangements, the social necessity, and others that I have presented. Like dependence on the weapon, without these adaptations none of us could have survived. But variability becomes a reasonable assumption. For we must have been few, right from the beginning, and our meager populations may well have been far scattered.

On no single stage, nor at some single time, did the human experiment begin. Here, there, another place, all along the retreating forest edge, certain ape populations proved better qualified than others to embark on the terrestrial adventure. A commitment here may have taken place a million years earlier than a commitment there, but the Pliocene was neither the time nor the place to encourage population explosions. So, wherever we were, we were few.

There is general agreement in anthropology that the members of a hunting society, early or late, could scarcely have exceeded fifty in number. That is about the maximum, including children, that the game on an available hunting range can supply. There is an informed guess, which naturally cannot be substantiated, that the hunting band consisted of more or less ten adult males. Much more would have meant too many dependents, too many mouths to feed, while significantly fewer could not have caught and killed those animals larger and faster than ourselves that we find in the fossil record.

Some readers may be aware of a consistent fallacy running through most of our anthropological literature. The "living fossil" fallacy is accepted by observers who take as their model contemporary hunting peoples to inform us as to our ways in ancient times. The Bushman and some Pygmies, for example, hunt frequently in twos. But they have not only the bow but the poisoned arrow, reducing risk for the hunter to a minimum. What is overlooked is that the bow-and-arrow, and the effective throwing spear as well, were not invented until about thirty thousand years ago. The long-distance weapon may be universally used today—a cultural step that I shall return to later on—but its spread was slow. Even when, at the end of the final glaciation, the American Indian entered the continent, though skilled in the use of a throwing spear with a fluted point, he did not have the bow-and-arrow. Nor did he receive it, so far as we know, until about fifteen hundred years ago.

Even thirty thousand years is the briefest of moments in the history of our hunting way, and only with great caution can we use the experience of contemporary hunters, however primitive, to illuminate the hunting techniques and social organization of earlier peoples who had somehow to survive without the aid of the weapon that could kill at a distance. The ancestral hunter had to face his prey with only two kinds of weapons. One was the handheld bludgeon or stabbing spear or hand ax or crushing stone; the other was the concerted action of his fellows. It was part of the story of cooperation that I considered earlier in this narrative. If group action failed, then individual risk was great. And at this point in my story the exclusive hunting range becomes significant. We faced enough dangers without competition from others of our kind.

Within biology, since the 1930's, the definition of a territory has been simply a defended area. The definition, inspired by G. K. Noble of the American Museum of Natural History, probably came about because by then new discoveries were revealing territory as a widespread, demonstrable fact of animal life, yet one of such variety of functions and characters that only the simplest of descriptions could be acceptable to all. When in 1966 I wrote *The Territorial Imperative,* introducing the concept to a larger public, I defined territory as an exclusive domain maintained and defended by an individual or a group against intrusion by members of their own species. Yet territory cannot be that simply disposed of. While an assertion of exclusive domain is a behavior pattern as ancient as lizards and bull-frogs and bad-tempered fish, its compulsions move some species and not others, and will even vary in a single species, such as the langur or the vervet monkey. Harvard's great biologist, Ernst Mayr, once put it to me this way: "If territory is of survival value, then you'll be territorial. If it isn't, you won't bother." And another of Harvard's great biologists, E. O. Wilson, has put it to me in another: "Territory is a set of behaviors independently evolved (and sometimes lost and re-evolved) of varying intensity and form, molded during relatively short periods of evolutionary time to meet particular environmental exigencies."

Arguments have been varied, lively, and valuable, since each tries to clarify a phenomenon more easily observed than explained. There are the diminishing ranks of those who would explain everything as learned, so that the young learn territorial animosity from their elders. Having watched precisely the same elaborate, formalized, territorial mating games performed by the Uganda kob at locations hundreds of miles apart, where they lack opportunity as much for the diffusion of learning as for the interchange of genes, I find the argument lacking persuasiveness. Of a different order is the interpretation of the German authority Paul Leyhausen, who sees territory as a geographical expression of dominance in which the proprietor gains status within his own preserve and so must fight for it, since he will lose his status anywhere else. There is much to be said for Leyhausen's simplification, just as there is much to be said for the suggestion, usually by ecologists—which I shall return to—that defense is an unnecessary portion of territorial behavior; that exclusivity is the point. According to this view the common baboon, who enjoys an exclusive range because no other baboons will intrude, is as much territorial as the gibbon who enjoys nothing so much as a good fight.

Whatever the variety of territorial interpretation, there is little variety in territorial expression. There is the same isolation on a private preserve, the same intolerance for neighbors. There is the same preoccupation with borders, the same invariable resistance to intrusion, and almost the same assurance that the intruder will be repelled. And so it was that in my earlier book I projected the thesis that man is a territorial species. We defend our space, our home, our village, our nation, not because we choose but because we must. Devotees of the all-is-learned school did not like it, of course. There are also those who are distressed by any "man-and-beast" association, but since they rarely read my books, they give me little trouble. Most readers, a bit stunned, inspected their own lifetimes of experience and muttered, "Well, so that was it. Of course." The ones who gave me a lasting problem—though the response might be surprising to those who approved—were the Marxists.

Yet the Marxist reaction was compulsory. If private property was a human invention which gave rise to the class struggle; if the state was created to protect the possessors from the dispossessed; and if the abolition of private property, as Lenin foresaw it, would lead to the withering away of the state (an event which has so far evaded the historical record): then the antiquity of territory presented a problem. Either fence-lizards, Canadian beavers, prairie dogs, three-spined stickleback fish, howling monkeys, defiant wildebeest bulls, intolerant female chameleons, warblers in variety, and gulls in variety were wrong—or Karl Marx was wrong. The latter conclusion was unthinkable. (Of passing interest was Marx's enchantment with Darwin, to whom he wanted to dedicate *Das Kapital*. Darwin was less enchanted.)

So I had a few political problems. And since it is all but impossible for the ideologically motivated scientist to conceive of conclusions that have come about through other than ideological motivation, I have a few problems still. But there was a more persuasive objection. If man is a territorial species, defending exclusive space not because he chooses but because he must, why isn't our most closely related species, the chimpanzee? Since this present investigation pursues the question, Why are we not chimpanzees? the question is not so much persuasive as interesting. And in 1966, when we were still unaware of how many primate species defend territory, the objection carried a certain force. We didn't know that much about primates, and we were only beginning to know about the chimp.

All of our early observations of the chimp, including those of Goodall, indicated a very loose social organization of smallish, shifting groups wandering about an unrestricted forestside quite lacking No Trespassing signs. When they encountered each other there was joy and stimulation, not the suspicion and hostility—veiled or overt—that we as human beings are accustomed to. Such a universal brotherhood of chimps lent hope for the brotherhood of man. It was all a bit too Rousseauesque for my stomach, and for my observations of universal social xenophobia in primates. Nor was it my stomach alone. Professor C. R. Carpenter, father of primate studies in the wild, once wondered to me if Goodall's chimps might be sick.

They were not sick. What some of us suspected, including Carpenter and Washburn, was that what seemed to be the warm embrace of chimpanzee strangers occurred in fact between the subgroups of a larger society of finite dimension. Goodall's great study was intensive; it was one of chimps as individuals. She was not approaching them with the broader, more superficial canvas of the social scientist. But such a study had to come.

It came. But since it was published in Japan in 1972 the study is not yet well known. For almost three years two Japanese scientists, Toshida Nishida and K. Kawanaka, staked out another, much larger area of mountain forest overlooking Lake Tanganyika. Their project had been inspired by the venerated founder of the Japanese Monkey Center, Junichiro Itani, who shared the suspicion that there was something so far unknown about chimpanzee social life. In their back-breaking domain the two Japanese found at least six distinct social groups that would have nothing to do with each other. They studied two intensively. One included about forty individuals; the other was much smaller. Yet there were barriers between them, lacking any geographical significance, that neither would cross except during seasonal periods of fruit shortage. Then the dominant group would occupy a portion of the other's terrain, and the subordinate would retreat. There was never an encounter, never a display—simply an avoidance that insured separation by at least a kilometer. The food shortage over, the dominant group would return to its established, exclusive range.

The chimp maintains an exclusive space and an exclusive society precisely as do so many other primates—the savannah baboon, the vervet monkey and langur under certain environmental conditions—not through conflict and defense but through avoidance. It is a primate precedent that hopefully man will catch on to some day. Since defense is a portion of the classic territorial definition, scientists, as I have implied, are divided as to whether or not this should be termed territorial behavior. It is not a question that I can settle, but the same end is accomplished. And one can see that in our transition from forest to savannah and our need for an exclusive hunting ground, little departure was necessary from chimpanzee territorial ways as we know them now.

At least at first. I have said that we hominids were few, just as the dwindling chimp is today. For a very long time, such was the immensity of African space, our social groups may have rarely made contact one with another. Avoidance was enough to insure a private hunting ground. A similar situation exists with the wolf, studied for so long by David Mech. All but exterminated by man, wolves are few, a pack's hunting ground large. Mech debated with himself whether they were territorial in the strict sense and concluded that they probably were. There is some evidence that they will defend their property, but not much, so seldom do strange wolves intrude.

Hunting in packs on the savannah, our conditions of survival became those of any other social predators—the wolf in the far north, the lion or hyena on our own savannah. All but the formidable African hunting dog maintain exclusive ranges, and he is an exception because he is so formidable. His hunting success is so much higher than any other predator that the presence of a pack in an area is enough to drive all potential prey out of the region. The late, great photographer Eliot Elisofon and I once stayed by a Serengeti pack for three days. We could not tell one species of gazelle from another without binoculars, since they remained so far away. Territory, for the hunting dog, is maladaptive. The pack must take its prey by surprise, continually moving long distances into areas where its presence has not yet been the subject of animal rumor.

Lion prides in the Serengeti will rigorously defend a territory of about fifty square miles, but population density is a factor of utmost significance to evolution. The great Ngorongoro caldera, rich with game, is the home of probably the world's densest collection of spotted hyenas. Hans Kruuk found there the cleanest distinctions of hyena clans, each with sharply defined territories so viciously defended that they became at times very nearly the subject of hyena wars. There were more than a few lethal conclusions—most unusual in territorial conflict. Yet on the broad Serengeti, with far more hyena elbow-room, such conflicts have seldom been observed.

The further back we go into a reconstructed human past and into the early limitations of a slowly adapting human foot, the more necessary it was that we found our game in a most limited hunting range. Napier's studies of the evolving foot, even two million years ago when we were slaughtering elephant and deinotherium, show that while we could run with all speed, we were still incapable of the stride necessary for long marches. And I am speaking of four million, six million, whatever millions of years ago. Yet we had some advantages. There was the innocence of animals, such as Paul Martin has described in North American prey pursued by skilled but unfamiliar intruders from Asia; our Pliocene victims could only have been easy marks. There was our ape brain, incomparably superior to that of any natural predator. If the relatively unintelligent lioness can practice tactical hunting and plan ambushes as Schaller has described, then our talents must have been of an order far beyond lion imagination. And there was another quite remarkable advantage: the Pliocene's desiccation. I myself have painted it as an interminable horror; but it was as cruel for other animals as for ourselves. The rare waterhole, the occasionally trickling stream, were the only places where they could come to drink. So water became a natural trap. We did not need the long-striding foot: we could wait with our ambush for the game to come to us.

And there was the final advantage that we were few. Valuable though a piece of real estate might be that boasted beckoning water, still we faced little competition from our kind. We had only, like the chimp or the baboon, to avoid each other to secure our exclusive rights. But while this meant isolation, we had to have neighbors on terms not too hostile. A social group of less than fifty is too small for continued breeding success. Since our young matured sexually at varying ages, and since there were unpredictable proportions of girls and boys, to keep a viable breeding population there had to be the occasional possibility of trading a surplus girl for a surplus boy. This shift of individuals in other primate species is almost invariably made by young males.

The exception, observed by the Japanese scientists, was the shift of young females between chimpanzee bands. This may have been the tendency among our early bands. So perhaps we traded, perhaps we raided. In any case, genetic necessity alone would have commanded a local population, as the word is used in biology: a larger interbreeding group of quite limited number but consisting of a small mosaic of fundamental social groups.

It was within the gene pool of such isolated populations that slow change and variation would come about. The change might be random—"genetic drift" in Sewall Wright's phrase—a strong force in totally isolated interbreeding populations. Or it might be a change of adaptation to local variations of environment. If we visualize this genetic landscape of the Pliocene emergence as one of far-separated islands of human advance, then it is not too difficult to understand why, when about three or four million years ago our fossil past comes at last into illumination, we find so many kinds of emerging beings.

Nor is it too difficult to understand why not only anatomical differences but behavioral differences were a product of varying inheritance. I have mentioned Kruuk's discovery of extreme territorial defense in the high-density population of spotted hyenas in the Ngorongoro crater. A similar variation between territorial avoidance and militant defense in relation to low or high population density has been studied in the langur in India and Ceylon. It cannot be unreasonable to suppose that in varying Pliocene environments there had been widely varying increases in population numbers over the long course of time. Here environmental pressure was so rigorous that populations became extinct; there, under conditions marginally endurable, life and death remained in such balance that populations were static; and over there, in a region of greater favor—such as Bishop described in northwestern Kenya—numbers slowly increased. But the society in relation to its hunting range could not increase much beyond the count of fifty. So increase meant subdivision, and hunting groups like the oldtime amoeba reproduced through division. Two groups emerged where one had been. This meant inflation in real estate values.

The competition for favored hunting grounds meant the renewal of the territorial imperative: to defend successfully what was yours became a matter of survival value. To surrender this waterhole, that little stream, this small lake, however undependable, was to perish. As Ernst Mayr so simply put it, if territory is to your survival advantage, you'll be territorial; otherwise you won't bother. And if Edward Wilson is correct, the pattern may evolve rather quickly. In the earliest days probably none of us needed to bother, we were so few. In later days all depended on this environment or that, on differing balances of death's equation. One back-bush population may have never faced the need; another, from a more numerous background, may have had for a million years the renewal of the territorial imperative.

So, as the Pliocene slowly relinquished its relentless grip, there emerged into our fossil horizon beings variously equipped to meet future contingencies. We may look at this fossil or that, this midget, that giant, but does it tell us the full story of behavioral equipment? How was this one equipped for competition? Did he have a compulsion to fight or to flee? We cannot know. But some survived and some did not, and one may reasonably guess that those who through expanding populations had the longest genetic history of selection for the territorial compulsion were better equipped, whatever their physical size, for the Pleistocene competition.

There is a corollary of the territorial imperative which in my earlier book I termed the amity-enmity complex. It is a rule—as easily illustrated in human as in animal history— that *probably* the greater the pressure of inimical force against a population, the greater will become the amity among social partners. There is nothing new about the concept, which has been discussed by social psychologists and practiced by every political leader who ever embarked on a foreign war to unite his quarreling people. What was new was the biological interpretation: just as the individual territorial proprietor experiences enhanced physiological capacities as he defends his domain, so group defenders experience enhanced cooperation and diminished devotion to self-interest. Had Adolf Hitler understood the sociobiology of Britain, I doubt that he would have sent his Luftwaffe against his enemy's territorial imperative; just as the Pentagon, had it known what it was doing, might have predicted with high probability that the American intrusion on Vietnamese soil would end up, whatever our might, with American disgrace.

The amity-enmity complex is a very real thing that no political scientists can neglect, despite its margin for error. What has never been reviewed, however—at least as far as I know—has been its possible contribution to human evolution and the social mind.

The phrase came up in London one noon-day while I was at lunch with that most impeccable yet imaginative of British anthropologists, Kenneth Oakley. He was coming down hard on the fixation that in our evolving past brain-size was all, and he was emphasizing that the individual size of brain was only one factor contributing to its competence. Total capacity could only be judged in terms of the pooling of brains towards a social end. He used the term *the social mind*. While, like the amity-enmity complex, equivalent concepts have entered many a meditation, in the biological sciences they are rare. Since Oakley's discussion, I myself have never seen the term used in the context which he projected.

As I write these paragraphs, I exercise the social mind. While I may inject an original conclusion or two, what I am dependent upon is a pool of experience gathered by thousands of scientific investigators. Without that pool, I am simply a man with a normal brain, a fairly high IQ, a fairly curious disposition, a moderate courage to swim against fashionable tides, and that is about all. Of utmost importance to me is the social mind. It is the switchboard that relays as it collects the signals from other brains.

What Oakley's observation confirmed was that throughout our evolving past, brain-size could mean only so much. Smaller brains could be effectively far superior to larger if they combined their efforts. And there would be a consequence. Once selection pressure rested on the effectiveness of the social mind, any advance in communication would have its selective value. More elaborate gestures and other nonverbal signals, rudimentary speech, refinement of language, the entrance of verbal symbols organizing speech and thought, memory and anticipation—a host of qualities that we associate with the human being had their roots in the survival necessities of the social mind.

While some scientists are quite correct, from an ecological point of view, in asserting that there is little difference between the holding of an exclusive group territory through avoidance or defense, psychologically they are far off base. The physical defense of a territory on the part of a hunting society meant a psychological union that the chimpanzee never knew. An appeal in the name of national security is a device we still use—legitimately or otherwise—to unite a people afflicted by domestic differences. Our old-time hunting societies may long since have vanished, but the amity-enmity complex still rests in the tool-kit of every politician, still remains as a social propensity of the human mind.

What I suggest is that those varying species of emerging hominids appearing on the fossil scene three or four million years ago varied not only anatomically, but also in their histories as territorial beings and their capacities for exerting the force of the social mind. We can have no fossil record except that of extinction. Nor have we the right to assume that territorial defense was everything in the shaping of that mind, for there was cooperative hunting as well and there was the demand for integration of sexually segregated yet mutually interdependent societies. Yet the amity-enmity complex was a powerful final force, unifying men, women, and children in its bond.

It is a truism of modern biology that anatomical change comes about *as a consequence* of behavioral change. And so I have chanted again and again the new refrain: "Birds do not fly because they have wings; they have wings because they fly." As it is with the wing, so it is with the brain. We do not think because our brain is big; our brain has grown big because we think. But I am not at this moment discussing the brain as an anatomical installation: rather, I am considering that far more elusive phenomenon, the mind. I believe that one can go beyond suggestion and firmly maintain that the human mind as we know it was a product of social necessity. It could never have come about in a species of fugitive apes. It would have presented limited advantage even to terrestrial hunters who, like the baboon, could always turn for survival to the individual scrounging of plant food. The human mind, with its infinite resources, could have come about only in a vulnerable species totally dependent on the hunt for survival, when with increasing numbers we faced the competition of our own kind, renewed the territorial imperative, pressed on into the inevitable areas of the amity-enmity complex, and through ruthless selection established the agglomeration of brain-power as the most potent, all-purpose tool we had ever known.

The human mind is the variable, extra-anatomical, immeasurable aspect of the standardized human brain, and it can act not at all according to animal laws of self-interest. Unlike the anatomical brain, it is a fraction of that larger entity, the social mind. And I doubt very much that it could ever have come to be without the selective pressures of the territorial imperative.

Eliot Howard was a British businessman and amateur ornithologist who discovered the territorial principle. I dedicated my own book to his memory, and shall not repeat myself here except for one most charming and illuminating of his observations in *Territory in Bird-Life* which he published in 1920. Despite his amateur standing, he had by that time established himself as the final scientific authority on warblers. In his book he ranged far beyond warblers in his observations; one species treated was the lapwing.

Howard's home was in Worcestershire, just above the River Severn. I myself have visited most of his vantage points of observation of birds on the moors, in the woodlands, on the ponds. Lapwings gathered low below the bluffs on the water meadows of the Severn. It is a countryside as lush as hearts human or lapwing might desire. In winter they gathered in sexually mixed congenial flocks, but with the sexual stirrings of springtime, things changed. Males, one at a time, separated themselves from the congenial flocks, on neutral grounds. Each went to establish elsewhere on the water-meadows a defended home of his own to which a property-conscious female would be attracted.

The winter of 1916, as Howard recalled it, was extremely severe and seemed to upset the breeding timetable. A mild spell would come; males would attempt to establish their territories; then frost and cold winds would disrupt hormonal arrangements and they would return to the friendly flock. Finally, one day in early March, two males had managed to get themselves permanently established. So now it was the flock that became confused, and instead of settling on its normal neutral ground, every lapwing came down on the two private territories. The males faced an extraordinary problem of defense, but they tackled it patiently. Fixing attention solely on one bird, the proprietor would confront it, display, and the intruder would fly off. He would go to the next, repeat his performance, and then on to another in turn. At last the two males could relax, their properties cleared.

The lapwing technique of handling a mob happens to be precisely that of the peaceable, traditional London bobby, who will go to one individual after another asking for names and addresses. It is the equivalent of lapwing display and, at least in older, less violent days, it had the equivalent effect. The crowd dwindled and cleared. Notable in the lapwing situation, even though territorial defense was strained, is the total absence of force.

The revival of territorial behavior in our evolving hunting societies meant by no means the coming of warfare. Howard's lapwing example gave a typical display of individual territorial defense not only in birdlife but, as thousands of observers since his original discovery have recorded it, in countless species. For mysterious physiological reasons the enhancement of energy and confidence that invests the proprietor on his familiar, definable terrain enables the ejection of an intruder—if not with simple display, then with a minimum of force.

For equally mysterious psychological reasons, many a critic of ethology seems incapable of grasping the exclusively defensive nature of territorial behavior. The object is never destruction of an intruder, merely his ejection. The object is never conquest of a portion of the next proprietor's space. In another book I have cited the only exception I know of in the animal world, observed by John King in his classic study of prairie dogs. Yet Erich Fromm, in his recent *Anatomy of Human Destructiveness,* can term "benign aggression" those forceful actions which we take to defend what is of survival necessity, while utterly failing to comprehend that the territorial imperative, as I have defined it here and as I explored it in my book, is precisely what he terms "benign aggression."

Our exclusive hunting territories were of survival necessity to our hunting ancestors. Right down to the time of our
earliest agricultural societies less than ten thousand years ago
there could have been as little motivation for conquest and
expansion as for taking a slave. The slave was another mouth
to feed; the acquisition of additional miles of range was
meaningless if we could not reach it. Even in a time of seasonal migration, when we may have moved our ranges to
keep up with the game, their size was severely limited by the
evolving capacities of the human foot. How far could we
go and return between sunrise and sunset? To leave a kill
on the savannah—or to leave ourselves there, for that matter—was an exercise in feeding our competitors, the nocturnal
predators.

I do not forget, however, that so long as we held a weapon
in our hands we were dangerous animals; it is as true of our
first savannah stirrings as it is of tomorrow night on a New
York street. Any of our quarrels over dominance, our tensions
between adults and maturing young, could have had a lethal,
if unpremeditated, conclusion. Nor do I neglect the conflicts
of raiding parties foraging for girls or boys of reproductive
age, or the lasting motives of revenge which such raids may
have initiated in others. Preambles for warfare they may
have been, but such conflicts were not of an essentially territorial nature. And so I cannot neglect the truly territorial
quarrels that came when a hungry, landless group attempted
to take over our range. These were the times, as I have suggested, when the stronger our genetic compulsion to defend
our space, and the more complete the union of the social
mind, the greater was our chance for survival. But from what
I have learned of territorial behavior throughout the animal
world I should suspect that lethal conflicts were few. The
advantages of the proprietor are too great. The landless intruder, following the same pattern of settlement so common
in our recorded history, would simply move on into the
empty spaces on the African map. This is perhaps how cer-

tain australopithecines, at precisely the same time in our history, wound up in South Africa. If they were less endowed than many of their northern contemporaries, then it would follow: they were losers. So it has been with many a relic people who have survived into the twentieth century through occupying the rain forest, the Arctic fringe, bleak Tierra del Fuego—real estate that no one else wanted.

There are many motives for territorial behavior, and one of ours—like that of any other social predator—was economic. Defense of the hunting range fell naturally on the males, the hunters. But there is another form of territory far more ancient, far more pervasive in the broad world of animal species, and that is the breeding territory. It is uncommon in primates, since apes and monkeys so seldom have a permanent home-site. But with our new way of life, defense of the breeding place resumed its ancient importance.

Let us think back for a moment, reviewing some of my suggestions concerning the new bipolar society. A principal problem facing the primate dependent on hunting was that our young took so long to grow up. We had none of the advantages of the natural predators. At a year the lion cub can follow a hunt. At six months the hunting-dog pups can keep up with the running pack, provided that it does not run too fast. In Southwest Africa I have watched a mother cheetah hunting, followed at a discreet distance by her remarkably large family, four cubs barely four months old. Such freedom was not for us. There had to be a place where infants could nurse, crawl, take their first steps, make their first little daring adventures away from their mothers, discover others of their age, play, form peer groups, run, chase and, as the years went by, assemble the skills and the experiences that in the distant future would qualify them as adult beings. And it had to be in a defended place.

In a bipolar society, divided throughout most of the daytime hours between the home and the hunting range, the defense of the living site fell naturally on the mothers. There would be older juveniles who could help, strong boys not yet sufficiently mature to join the hunters. Such juveniles make a significant contribution to the defenses of a baboon troop. In hazardous areas haunted by such diurnal predators as the ancestral cheetah or occasional lion, human necessity may have dictated that a male or two was less valuable on the hunt than at home standing guard. But whatever her assistance, it was the female who became the principal guardian of the home, just as she remains to this day.

Sexual dimorphism is the biological term for the physical differences between male and female within a species. In some species like the gibbon and the elephant and the herring gull there is so little difference in size and marking that the untrained eye has difficulty making a distinction. In most apes and monkeys, however, the male is by far the larger and more powerful. You and I may look on sexual dimorphism in the human species as marked, but from a chimp's-eye view it would probably not seem too striking. I suspect, though I cannot prove, that in our savannah life, selective demands for strong females changed the direction of primate tendency.

What is remarkable, though quite understandable, is that sexual dimorphism came to characterize our territorial dispositions. Intrusion into our economic territory inflamed the territorial imperative in the male. And for all we know this may account for the lingering male resistance to the intrusions of capable, ambitious females into our traditionally male economic territories of business and government and labor jurisdictions. Whether it is true or not, certainly the opposite side of the territorial coin is evident: the implacable defense of that breeding site known as the home by the female proprietor against the intrusions of neighbors, other females, even husbands. It is an innocent observer who believes that the female is less aggressive than the male;

she is merely aggressive about different things. And she can be as brutal as any male.

I do not imply, however, that defense of the breeding territory was ever left solely to the mothers. It is concerned far too intimately with the security of the young and reproductive success. There is a universal observation of territorial behavior in animal species that—while intrusion may meet a degree of toleration at the borders of a range, so that boundaries may even overlap—the closer the intruder penetrates the heartland, the more intolerant become the defenders. Sir Julian Huxley once described a territory as like a rubber disc which, the more firmly squeezed, the more firmly it resists. It is a characteristic that surprisingly enough has left its mark on our legal systems. While cultures may differ, the sanctity of the home has a widespread acceptance, and among predominantly Anglo-Saxon cultures has legal support verging on the shocking.

I am grateful to Dean Peter Brett of the University of Melbourne's law school for examples quite beyond my own technical capacities for research. In Britain, for example, there was a case known as R. v. Hussey in 1924. Mr. Hussey, with his family, rented a room from a landlady named Mrs. West. She claimed that she gave him oral notice to leave. He refused, claiming that it was not a valid notice, and barricaded his door. Mrs. West and her friends armed themselves with hammer, chisel, and poker, and succeeded in breaking a panel of the door. He fired, wounding her friend, a Mrs. Gould. He was convicted at the Old Bailey of "unlawful wounding." He appealed. He was set free. The decision rested on an old tradition in English law that in self-defense you have no right to use force unless you retreat, but "that in defending his home he need not retreat . . . for that would be giving up his house to his adversary."

The decision raised a considerable hubbub of alarms in the legal profession, since it set what seemed to be the value of property above the value of human life. Yet to Brett's knowledge the decision has never been reversed, and an American experience seems to confirm it.

Earlier, in 1914, a murder case came up before the New York Court of Appeals. Benjamin Cardozo—who in later years, when a Supreme Court Justice, would become an immortal in American legal history as a rare intellect, liberal, and humanist—wrote the opinion of acquittal. In part he recorded:

> It is not now and never has been the law that a man assailed in his own dwelling is bound to retreat. If assailed there he may stand his ground and resist the attack. He is under no duty to take to the fields and the highways, a fugitive from his own home. . . . Flight is for sanctuary and shelter, and shelter if not sanctuary is in the home.

In 1962 the American Law Institute went to work on a recommendation to unify the varying American legal codes in our fifty separate states. When the Institute came to this point it agreed, as English law had anticipated, that in simple self-defense the use of deadly force must be justified in terms of threat and impossible retreat. But they agreed that the "actor" is not obliged to retreat from his dwelling place unless it is established that he was the aggressor in the first place. According to Brett, the recommendation was accepted without argument, on an "everybody knows" basis. In Brett's acid terms, while all of the recommendations to our various states were debated and accepted on "rational" grounds, there is little doubt that the legal conclusions rested simply on our subconscious acceptance of the biological animal law known as the territorial imperative.

And so it came to be that an ancient animal law, the defense of exclusive space, was revived by a primate invading the vast African savannah. We had our primate problems: slow feet, slow-growing young. We solved them, or there would be no inheritor *Homo sapiens*. We solved the problems through life and death, through the extinction of this population, the survival of that, the superior genetical endowment through long selection of these, the passing over of those. The fossil bones leave an ambiguous record. We can only speculate on the differing views of the world of the ape-brained varying beings who would contribute or fail to contribute to our genetic inheritance.

What we can guess, with fair authority, was that the male, viewing from a hilltop the Texas-like space of Africa, saw it one way; the female, viewing the antics of her children in a quite different geographical perspective, saw it another. Again and again I must reassert that had not both males and females, each in their own way, relighted the fires of the ancient territorial imperative, the human being would not exist.

The Cultural Animal

A gull called the kittiwake very long ago made what many would describe as a cultural advance. This set in motion a long series of biological adaptations that would never have occurred except for the peculiar nature of the cultural step.

Purists may object to the use of the term *culture* to refer to any but the achievements of a thinking being capable of choice. Perhaps they are right, even though such purism, to my ear, smacks of anthropocentrism. We have seen in our history how a single cultural step—dependence on a tool called the weapon—brought about, among other biological consequences, the loss of our primate fighting teeth. But I can't believe that at this remote stage in our evolution such an undoubted cultural acquisition was accomplished by a being who was much of a thinker, or whose new way of life left him much choice.

Whatever my reservations, however, a semantic problem remains. I may regard as a cultural advance any action taken by any animal to modify the environment to suit his needs, in contrast to the normal biological adaptation encouraging changes in the organism to meet environmental demands. Yet that is not how we use the term, so I shall speak of *protoculture* in reference to animal achievement.

The kittiwake spends most of its life far out at sea, returning to land only for breeding. Defense of the nest and the young has encouraged in most birds a powerful territorial intolerance. Unlike other gulls, who normally nest in large colonies on open ground, the kittiwake found a remarkable ecological niche that offered all but invulnerable natural defense. The kittiwake nests on tiny ledges in cliffs so steep that no one, not even the predatory herring gull, can get at them. The ledges may be as narrow as four inches, the narrower the better. But the nesting sites on such uneven, broken, sometimes crumbling ledges would have been impractical except for the protocultural achievement.

Almost twenty years ago one of Niko Tinbergen's students at Oxford, Ellen Cullen, studied the kittiwake on certain island cliffs off the Northumberland coast. How she got at them I don't know, but it is one of the most elegant and significant studies in ethological literature. The kittiwake pair collect mud, grass, roots, and seaweed to make a firm cement. Bringing it to their ledge in their beaks, they slap it on like mortar with sidewise flips of their heads, then trample it flat with their feet. So they extend the ledge where it is too narrow or crumbles away, flatten it where it is too uneven. They finish off their platform with a deep cup from which the eggs cannot roll out.

The biological consequences of this triumph of kittiwake engineering have been almost innumerable. Defense is so perfect that there is no need for camouflage. Among gull species that nest on the open vulnerable ground, for example, the chicks are invariably of a cryptic color difficult to spot if you are a hungry hawk. Kittiwake chicks are brightly marked with a gray back and white throat and underside. Within a few days after hatching the chicks of ground-nesting gulls leave the nest to defecate. There is no room for such a performance on the kittiwake ledge, nor is there need. The chicks perch on the edge of the nest and defecate over the edge, accumulating a tell-tale white ring around each nest, of no importance since camouflage is unnecessary. So safe do the birds feel in their kittiwake-constructed castles that, unlike other gulls, they have only the rarest alarm-call. Out in the open, on the beach perhaps, they are so nervous that an observer can approach them no closer than forty yards. But in their nests, according to Cullen, one can almost touch them.

Raising a family in a space so tiny presents problems. Other gulls, when young, start flying with ample time for practice. Young kittiwakes at the age of six weeks must simply take off, and fly or fall. All gulls feed their young by regurgitation on the ground, where the chicks peck it up. Since kittiwakes have no such room, the young must take their meals directly from the parents' throats. The parents, without room for maneuver, cannot even copulate properly, so she makes ready by sitting down.

There is not even room for proper quarreling. Herring gulls are a belligerent lot, and while their territories in a colony are small, there is still room for proper pecking and wing-beating. Not so the kittiwake. Therefore, they have perfected beak-to-beak fighting not unlike swordsmen's dueling. There comes a moment when, if you are losing, you would normally signal the victor by retreating. But there is nowhere to retreat. What do you do? You sheathe your sword; you hide your beak under your wing. To reinforce the appeasement signal, there is a little black line of feathers across the back of the neck that rises and becomes visible when you so duck your head. Among forty-four species of gull, Cullen found this line only in the kittiwake.

So a single protocultural achievement has brought on a chain of biological adaptations, behavioral or anatomical, that would be of no survival significance but for the kittiwake's unique way of life. That the engineering capacity with consequent superior defense was of significant survival value may be read in the success of kittiwake child-raising. Among herring gulls only 40–50 percent of the chicks live to fly away from home; in three seasons of observation, Cullen found a startling kittiwake record of 88 percent. So high is the survival rate that it would bring on a population problem, with cliff sites for nesting few. Therefore we have kittiwake birth control. While the pair could raise three chicks with ease, in 75 percent of nests clutch-size is limited to two.

The kittiwake is by no means unique in boasting such an accomplishment as part of its survival kit. All nests may be so described. Wart hogs have their burrows, prairie dogs their underground labyrinths, beavers their dams and their lodges. The weaver bird hangs its complex cylindrical nests like Christmas ornaments in a convenient tree, and in Southwest Africa I have seen a species that builds, communally, a single large woven mass with countless entrances to individual apartments. Such protocultural achievements are of no mean order, and though I know of none to compare with the kittiwake in complexity of biological consequence, still we have the beaver and its tail, blind moles with their specialized digging feet.

All in the broad sense are cultural animals in that they command a means of adapting the environment to their needs, though it may be the better part of scientific wisdom to exclude from the concept of culture such programmed, genetically directed behaviors. We shall find ourselves in difficulty, however. There is no great difference between a mode of action learned from social tradition and another directed by innate compulsion. Social tradition is more flexible, more quickly acquired than the long wait for genetic fixation. Many an animal combines them both. Konrad Lorenz's famous jackdaws—small European editions of the crow family—have no instinctual recognition of natural enemies. There is simply a warning cry on the part of the flock based on past experience that informs every naïve individual about danger. So a man with a gun may need no ancient menace to inspire jackdaw apprehension. Further away from jackdaw instinctual response to the warning cry are comparable experiences with baboons by both the modern authority Irven DeVore and Eugène Marais, South Africa's eccentric pioneer of ethology at the turn of the century. Both have recorded the social response to gunfire. DeVore's experience came about in Nairobi's protected reserve, where no shooting could have contributed to baboon experience for at least a human generation. For excellent reasons of physiological inspection, scientists shot two baboons. By no means all of the troop was present, yet for at least a year all became unapproachable by humans.

Marais's experience came about after the Boer War. For years the farmers had been away fighting, and most of their elders and women and children condemned to Kitchener's concentration camps. The baboons had a holiday of theft from diminishing orchards and fields. The war ended, but for years afterward the defeated Afrikaners were denied weapons. Then at last on a farm came two farmers with guns. Old baboons with old memories barked their warning. The curious young, ignoring the warnings, hung back to inspect the strangers. Two young females were killed. It was the end in that district of man-baboon accord.

I should myself interpret the baboon response not at all to instinct but to the experience of elders and the commands of the social mind. If we do not understand it, then let us not neglect it. In a primate as advanced as the baboon the social mind communicates the experience of the few to the survival advantage of the many. David Mech's observations of the wolf on Isle Royale, in Lake Superior, produced a striking photograph from the air of the pack, after testing a moose, in a nose-to-nose huddle "deciding" whether to attack or to move on to a moose less dangerous. No more decision was involved than that of American football players in a similar huddle taking their signals from the quarterback. Wolves, like their descendant dogs, have an inborn need for a leader. Their quarterback was the alpha male, presumably the most experienced. His was the decision that this moose was bad medicine, so they obediently moved on. How they had communicated, we do not know.

Such powers of the wolf and the savannah baboon in times before verbal language must unquestionably have been a portion of our inherited mental jurisdiction. And so, if just one of our early fellows picked up a natural wooden bludgeon to fend off a hyena or smash the brains of a prey, the news would have quickly spread. The event may have taken place in a thousand places at a thousand times. The acquisition of a new means of defense or attack, through extension of arm and hand by means of a tool which we call the weapon, would have rapidly become not the secret of the experienced few but, through the social mind, the possession of all.

I call the human being a cultural animal not because we "invented" the weapon and became dependent upon it. A prairie-dog town is dependent on holes in the ground. What distinguishes our kind is that once we set in motion a cultural advance, because of biological consequences we could not go back. The consequences might be varied. Loss of our fighting teeth meant that we could not go back to a world without weapons. It did not, however, deny us a return to the trees for food and protection. But the weapon, even though it may have first come about as a defensive tool, meant a facility that chimps and baboons had never known. Greater and greater dependence on meat-eating and the hunting way meant another cultural advance—"cultural" in the strict sense, since it was a matter of choice or tradition so long as we could still go back to the trees. But then came the biological consequence of the flattening, terrestrial foot. Choice was denied us.

We became biological prisoners of cultural advances. In previous chapters I have described what must have been some of the novel cultural consequences, unknown in the vegetarian primate, that had to come about with our new biological limitation: food-sharing, the male role of provider, the bipolar society in part sexually segregated, the female role of defender of the home-site. But cultural change had in turn its biological consequences. I have discussed at length the radical physiological rearrangements in the sexual capacities of the evolving human female, which I myself cannot see as of any selective value except in societies as culturally unique as our own. Handedness was another, the specialization of skill in one hand at the cost of the other. It was no simple matter of practice or conditioning, since handedness depends on a complex neural circuitry in the brain giving one hemisphere dominance over the other. If you are right-handed, then your skill is mediated by motor centers in your brain's left hemisphere.

Ambidextrousness is as uncommon in human beings as it is common in other primates. The advantage of handedness must be obvious in hunters' swinging clubs or throwing stones for a living. The advantage could only have been much enhanced when we came into an era of skilled tool-making. But I find it doubtful indeed to believe that such a complex neurophysiological arrangement came about *after* the brain's enlargement. It was one, and just one, of those pressures inherited from our small-brained days that made a more elaborate neocortex of selective advantage and contributed to the new brain's structure.

As we come to the three-million-year horizon in our evolution, with the harsh Pliocene beginning to fade from our experience, we find the cultural animal so far advanced that already he is making stone tools. Not only was he making them, but at Lake Rudolf he was making them so skillfully as to throw a disturbance into the Leakey family. What was wrong? A million years older, some were better made than the vast assemblage of tools found by the elder Leakeys in the earliest deposits of the Olduvai Gorge. Mary Leakey took her doubts to London to consult Kenneth Oakley at the British Museum. Oakley solved it. At Olduvai the common materials were lava and quartz, most difficult to work. At Rudolf our ambitious craftsmen had a fine-grained volcanic material called *trachyandesite,* far easier to fashion. But nothing about the explanation refuted the skill of hand that we possessed three million years ago.

Few of these early stone implements from East Africa, whether a million or three million years old, should be regarded as weapons. They were fairly small. It is true that in my Chicago youth, whatever the incidence of machine guns in violin cases, the gangster's favorite weapon was the blackjack, a leather-coated piece of lead so small that you could conceal it in your hand, yet which when properly wielded could crush a skull. It is also true that at Olduvai one finds the *spheroid,* an implement most difficult to explain as other than a weapon. It is round, about the size of a baseball, and painstakingly chipped. One's first interpretation might be that a missile perfectly round could be thrown with greater accuracy than an ordinary stone. But as Mary Leakey has concluded, if used in such fashion so many would be lost as to reduce perfect chipping to a waste of time. Louis Leakey thought that he had tended to find them in threes, and suggested that they had been used like the Argentine *bola.* The gaucho, instead of using the lasso, captures a steer with several stones connected by rope which, whirling, entangle the animal's legs. Most critics, feeling that the technology was a bit advanced for the early Pleistocene, greeted the suggestion with reserve. But son Richard Leakey has demonstrated that just two of the spheroids, connected by a thong, will wrap themselves tightly about a post or tree. We do not know what these missiles were, but undoubtedly they were weapons. And we are learning not to underrate the ancient capacities of the evolving cultural animal.

Nevertheless, the early stone implements seem mostly to have been small cutting tools. The multitude found mixed

136

with the skeleton of a two-million-year-old elephant seem most unlikely to have been used to kill him, but certainly were used to butcher him. If you have ever tried to chew your way through an elephant's hide, then you can appreciate the need of skilled hunters for surgical instruments. There seems to have been no urgent need for improvement of weapons. Raymond Dart made an impressive demonstration of the selective use of animal bones as weapons in the hands of his South African australopithecines. While we may well have done the same in our earlier Pliocene years, still our East African family, even when we first find it, was a long cultural stage ahead of the South African suburbanites. I suspect, from the uncounted number of our early cutting and chopping tools, that many were used for shaping and pointing wooden spears. Hand-held, the spears were deadly enough weapons for hunting demand.

What was happening to the cultural animal can by no means be confined to the skills of his hands as he developed efficient techniques for shaping stone artifacts. Nor can it be confined to inevitable—and as it turned out irreversible—social change in the direction of division of labor. Some individuals must have proved themselves more skillful than others, more patient than others, when confronted with the delicacies of chipping stones. The gross division between hunters and mothers began to break down. Individual talents—often, surely, the talents of women—rose in social value. But the most significant thing that was happening was to the mind.

Many an animal can adapt a portion of his environment to his needs. The chimp can take a twig, strip it of leaves, and use it to fish termites from a mound. He has truly made a tool. But when we took a stone and chipped it into a pattern that would suit our needs, then we created something that does not exist in nature. We were fashioning something to a design existing only in our own minds.

The story of man has several critical turning points, and

this is one of them. We had been cultural animals certainly for some millions of years, continually dependent on cultural acquisitions for survival. We had become animals quite unique in that the biological changes that came about in consequence of cultural advance forbade retreat. But as notable as the opportunities presented to our unique, advancing being was the imprisonment that our cultural-biological changes brought about. We could do this; we could no longer do that. We could go here, we could no longer go there. New environments opened before us; they remained our masters, however, since they contained us. Now something new happened.

If you go back to our earliest pebble-tools, you find that we took a quite ordinary stone, perhaps from a riverbed, that suited our hand and chipped off a cutting edge along one side. We modified, like the chimp his twig, something that we found in nature. I think that future discovery will reveal such tools four and five million years old. Our chipping progressed very, very slowly. The record at Olduvai is clear. We made finer chips. We produced "bifacials" chipped on both sides. But not till about a million and a half years ago did we turn out such creations as the spheroid from mental designs divorced from the suggestions of nature.

I often used to wonder why the human brain took such an immense span of years to expand significantly from ape-sized endowment. As compared with the way of the chimpanzee in his fruitful, sheltering forest, ours became a way of infinite intellectual challenge. We had to learn so much. We had to learn about so many varying species of game, the trails they frequented, their different manners of defense. We had to learn about seasons and migrations, even the likeliest hours of the day that species would appear, and the unlikeliest—as at midday—when they would vanish. We had to learn about predators, too, and how there is little to fear in the well-fed lion and much to fear in the hunting dog, but only at dawn and dusk. Above all we had to find means of inhibition in this brain of ours on behalf of risk-taking and cooperation, and deferred reward. The survival necessity of bringing the meat back home was a shattering development in the psyche of the primate male.

Perhaps it took millions of years just to reorganize the circuitry of the old ape-brain without visible effects on the fossil record. Surely Oakley was right about the social mind: you did not need a bigger brain if through a compound of capacities you made more effective use of the brain you had. Nevertheless, something at last began to happen, and it happened only *after* we began to shape nature to our own designs.

As you go through the long history of our artifacts, you will come on something quite recognizably new, the Acheulian culture. The suggestions of nature are entirely ignored. The characteristic Acheulian hand ax is almond-shaped, symmetrical, chipped with care on both sides; examples differ little whether found in the Thames valley or at the ends of Africa. For hundreds of thousands of years it so dominated the rubbish heaps of our history that it became known as the Boy Scout knife of the ancient world. It was an all-purpose tool.

Hand-held, it was a far deadlier weapon than the blackjack so beloved by Chicago's gangsters. Some of our earlier choppers and spheroids may have had their lethal uses. An early Hungarian, Vértesszöllős man, had his head caved in a few hundred thousand years ago by an inferior chopper found beside him. It worked. But with the Acheulian hand ax we perfected our first specialized, inarguable stone weapon, and since it became so popular, there is little wonder. Yet it was not that specialized, for while it may have been a bit clumsy for picking your teeth, still it had its uses for cutting open a tough-skinned animal, or as a scraper for cleaning a hide.

139

The Acheulian hand ax, however, tells much more about how we were. Not only in its pure design was it a triumph of what man had in mind over what nature provided; it also meant the coming of style. The social mind was becoming larger than the isolated traditions of a social group. If you found in earlier times artifacts resembling those at remote sites, no contact was implied. It meant little more than that skilled workers, taking their cues from natural objects universally available to provide a cutting tool of universal necessity, came independently to about the same answer. But the almond-shaped hand ax was so irrelevant in terms of natural suggestion and, wherever found, it was so uniform in design and technique of making, that some kind of human contact seems inevitable. For thousands or tens of thousands of years various peoples may have carried on the traditions of the social mind, but somewhere in their history there must have been outside contact and imitation.

The suggestion may seem wild that with the Acheulian hand ax we are seeing the foundation of what we regard as both technology and art. I am not alone, however, in this conclusion. For there was something else about the hand ax— it was *unnecessarily beautiful*. Its symmetry, its delicacy of workmanship, go far beyond functional demand. A much cruder instrument, much more easily made, would have been just as effective. Why did we go to all the trouble?

In the days when we looked to the big brain for the origins of all things human, we naturally assumed that the discovery of an Acheulian culture meant that men of approximately our endowment had been around. The early discovery of Pekin man in the caves at Choukuotien reinforced the assumption. Our brain-size today ranges about fifteen hundred cubic centimeters or, let us say, three pints. Pekin man had a two-pint brain, about midway in development between the australopithecines and ourselves. But Pekin man did not have the Acheulian culture, and a problem emerges for which I have no answer.

We today classify these two-pint halfway houses as racial variants of the species *Homo erectus*. Representatives include not only Pekin man, but the earlier *Pithecanthropus* from Java; from the West, one from Ternifine in Algeria; other ones from Olduvai and South Africa; several from Europe, such as Swanscombe in England, Heidelberg in Germany, and Vértesszöllős in Hungary. The only question mark concerning any of them is how far they were progressing towards the status of *Homo sapiens*. All bear much the same age, towards a half-million years. I recall being Philip Tobias's enthusiastic, if amateur, witness to the measurement of the cranial capacity of the Olduvai example. The result, 980 cubic centimeters, was precisely the same as a Java specimen. No non-anatomist could have distinguished between the two or doubted their common earlier ancestry. Yet there is a clinker.

In Java, from a much earlier date, a definitely hominid fossil was discovered at Modjokerto. Authorities have debated, Was it an australopithecine? Then, perhaps two million years ago, the australopithecines must have moved into Asia. Since we now know the immense antiquity of the australopithecines in Africa, there is no sound reason to believe that they may not have moved through the warm tropical world as far as Java. But was it then an ancestor of a separately evolving group of *erectus*, exemplified later by Java and Pekin man? There is the evidence on the one hand that the African-based Acheulian culture never reached Asia. And there is the evidence on the other hand, which I myself witnessed, that contemporary examples of *erectus* from East Africa and Java, and China as well, are virtually indistinguishable. I find it difficult to accept convergent evolution of such an order, yet even more difficult to penetrate the mystery. Gladly I may turn to another.

We had long assumed that such an invention as the almond-shaped hand ax must have proceeded from a fairly modern being. Then, to everybody's shock, Mary Leakey came up with Olduvai evidence that about 700,000 years ago the famous hand ax was being made by *erectus* with the two-pint brain. The 700,000-year marker is of very great importance the world around, since at that date the magnetic poles reversed. Before that date your compass would have pointed south, afterwards north, and the record was left in the crystallization of volcanic materials. Mary Leakey's discovery of an Acheulian hand ax seems to come from a period of reversed polarity, when the compass pointed south. If so, then the date could not be later than 700,000 years. But her discovery has been confirmed by another demonstrating the very great Acheulian antiquity.

In mid-1974 two of our most knowledgeable, responsible workers in the field of African origins published a paper in *Nature* magazine. One is Glynn Isaac, who recently has been working with Richard Leakey on the Lake Rudolf discoveries, but who through the years has established himself as a high authority on the Acheulian industry. The other is G. H. Curtis, who with J. F. Evernden fathered the technique of absolute dating through the steady decay of an isotope of potassium into argon. They had investigated an undoubted but very early Acheulian deposit near Lake Natron, fifty miles from Olduvai. Curtis had his potassium-argon dates, but the results were so staggering that they turned to geomagnetic reversals for confirmation. The Acheulian industry occurred in a period of *negative* (South Pole) polarity but between two short periods of positive polarity, the later of which could not have been a part of the modern era. The geophysicists have these two short-lived switches of polarity nailed down. This Acheulian industry had to be somewhere between a million and a million and a half years ago.

In terms of the cultural animal, the fall-out of this discovery lies beyond prediction. Mary Leakey's discovery was enough to demonstrate that the Acheulian invention, so superior to anything that had come before, had nothing to do with the modern human brain, and that it probably originated in East Africa. The Isaac-Curtis discovery confirms this so emphatically as to introduce new enigmas. Who *did* author the Acheulian advance? We have found so far no fossil record of the presence of even two-pint *Homo erectus* at such an age. The record of nearby Olduvai is fairly complete, so—in simplified detective-story terms—whodunit? It would be good to be a twenty-year-old anthropologist with such an event to investigate. The answer could be a long time coming.

The authors of this paper present a proper question, however, regarding our present status as human beings. Why—if the Acheulian cultural capacity began to appear so very long ago—why did it not appear elsewhere in the Old World until at the very most half a million years ago? We may wonder about Pekin man and the Asian branch of our two-pint species, and his failure to adopt the superior culture of our African Acheulians. The question that the authors of the paper properly ask is why, with such a cultural advance, we didn't very soon spread out of the East African heartland all around the Old World. But we did not. Glynn Isaac once made a long study of a site near Nairobi called Olorgesailie, which I described in *The Social Contract*. It is mature Acheulian, with the inexplicably beautiful hand axes such as I have described, and it is 400,000 years old. Yet even then we have very little trace of the culture outside of Africa.

Why is it that our ancestral species of true *Homo*, with such cultural talent, took so long to break out of the tropical heartland? The very earliest record is not in Europe but in Israel, at a site high above the Jordan River, not far from the Sea of Galilee. Perhaps these were pioneers moving along an obvious migration route. The site is known as Ubeidiya, and it is so old that the Jordan Valley has fallen in since, and what was once a level living site now stands at an angle of seventy degrees. Here you find spheroid missiles in number, and a less developed Acheulian culture than at Olorgesailie but quite in accord with its age—650,000 years. Significantly, you find no trace of fire.

What I believe held us back from any movement into the colder regions of the world was our lack of fire. It was not just that we did not know how to make it; we did not understand it. Perhaps because we had evolved in an equatorial climate where the value of a fire's warmth meant little in terms of survival, for all our skills the concept of fire as a friend eluded us. When the discovery at last was made, then the cultural animal could take a stride as long as from Kenya to Britain. The deepening cold of the early Ice Age had inhibited any northern advance. The advent of Acheulian techniques had meant nothing: what was a hand ax against the blizzard? Fire was the answer. The discovery of its value could have been made by any people at any time, and if its discovery in both Europe and Asia was made at about the same time, it was because of the simultaneous challenge of the Ice Age threat. But of course the discovery was irreversible, since we came to live in lands where without fire we would have perished.

Fire became, from the time of *Homo erectus* until today or tomorrow, the theme song of the cultural animal. When we concern ourselves with the energy crisis, we sing an old, old tune.

I find it difficult to believe that in tropical Africa we had no experience of the value of fire to the hunt. Clark Howell, in Spain, found inarguable evidence that *Homo erectus,* three hundred thousand years ago, used fire to drive elephants into a concentrated area convenient for killing and butchering. In the days of the Belgian Congo I found notable evidence of the incidence of natural grass-fires. The Belgian naturalists who supervised the great Parc Albert demanded that everything be natural. In most African game reserves the dried grass is fired to clear the way for fresh grasses to delight their grazing citizens. The Belgians found that if you left it to lightning storms, every corner of the reserve would be burned over in the course of three years. Leopards understand, and maribou storks, and they congregate wherever there is a grass fire to fatten themselves on small fleeing animals and insects. If they can understand, then I cannot believe that our imaginative ancestors did not.

Yet evidence exists in plenty that in warm Africa, until a hundred thousand years ago at most, we did not have hearths. Future discovery may rearrange the scene. Raymond Dart once believed that his australopithecines at the South African site of Makapan used fire, and so he gave his small-brained beings the new name *Australopithecus prometheus*. His evidence has been discredited. What we know of the early history of fire has been entirely gained from cold Europe and Asia.

I have discussed the origins of fire quite briefly in terms of the origin of cooking. Authorities agree that before forty or fifty thousand years ago few of us knew how to make fire, and so we could depend on cooking. This is a mere yesterday. Nevertheless you find hearths associated with *Homo erectus* at far earlier dates. Again there is general agreement that while we did not know how to make fire, we knew its value, and we could capture natural fire as regularly as I have described my experience in the Belgian Congo. Yet we have no evidence so far acquired to indicate significant use of fire in Africa at that time, nor for a very long time to come. Why then, in the early stages of the Ice Age, did some of us wander away from our warm African womb to enter northern regions just when they were developing the most appallingly unfavorable climatic conditions? If we skip such a question, we are ignoring a most fundamental paradox in the evolving human animal.

At the time of the Israel discovery, the Ice Age was only beginning its moderate advance. The Arctic seems to have frozen over for the first time 700,000 years ago, that memorable date when the poles reversed. This was just before the Ubeidiya discovery, where we find no evidence of fire. Shortly afterward came the first wave of European glaciation, a relatively minor event, followed by an interlude not too intolerable. There is evidence that Heidelberg man may have appeared in Germany in this period, and Acheulian artifacts have been found in England. Strangely enough, it is not until the second and most savage of the ice sheets, Mindel, that we begin to find the conclusive and far-flung evidence of the spread of *Homo erectus* through cold Eurasia. Not even rodents could take it, and many a species became extinct. Yet here we were, tropical beings, pressing on through the endless winters and brief summers of Mindel and of the cold, dry interglacial that was to follow.

We find their hearths in China, in Hungary, near the mouth of the Rhône. Life without fire would seem to have been impossible. Within walking distance of the harbor at Nice, Henry de Lumley, the French archaeologist, has found, three hundred thousand years old, not only hearths but the certain evidence for a building with a wooden frame. It is our first known structure. It was about the same date as Howell's elephant-hunters in Spain who used fire to drive their giant prey into a bog for slaughter. (It was an extinct, straight-tusked species larger than the African elephant.) We did all right. In contemporary caves at Choukuotien are thousands of bones, probably of an ancestral reindeer, and times were cold.

But why did we come north at such an impractical season? Well, there is one practical answer: that hunting was good. And if we think back once again to Paul Martin's North American overkill of naïve animals, I find it not unreasonable to suppose that able, well-armed Acheulian man in East Africa was having a bit of trouble with his prey. They were getting wary of us, developing in their own instinctual

146

equipment what we now call flight distance. Eurasian prey—deer, horses, ancestral cattle—had never seen men before. They had not evolved side by side over the millions of African years with these small, infinitely dangerous beings. So perhaps that was it, and we found on these northern steppes hunting grounds so rich that, despite the wretched climate, we never went back to Africa.

But just possibly there was a less practical side to the sudden wanderings of our two-pint ancestor. I have mentioned that this was the time, more or less half a million years ago, when the African-born Acheulian hand ax reached its full development of technical perfection and unnecessary beauty. Our success as hunters, together with a relaxing climate, division of labor, and the emergence of the artisan role, meant a social tolerance, if not even social prestige, for the superior artisan. No longer was it quite so necessary for the male to prove himself as a superior hunter before boy could gain girl. No longer perhaps was it necessary for a woman of skill and imagination to establish a reputation as the best sexual opportunity in camp. There was another road, and it was the road of art.

I am taking this guessing game farther back than any substantial evidence. It would be a good half-million years until Imhotep, the first architect in recorded history, designed in Egypt the step pyramid at Saqqara five thousand years ago. So we must not get carried away by speculations concerning two-pint devotees of art for art's sake. Yet there is a peculiar coincidence in the cultural animal's inclination to design hunting weapons more pleasing than necessary. This was happening not only in the African heartland, with the Acheulian hand ax. A shade of time later it was happening also in China.

I have mentioned that at Choukuotien, the ancient cave-deposits of Pekin man, there is no trace of the Acheulian tradition. We do not know why. It is a culture that for part of its history seems to have developed independently from the African tradition. So they stuck to the older, more Olduvan disposition of cleavers and cutting tools. But there was something odd. Easily worked chert was immediately available in the area of the caves. Yet they insisted, time and again, on making tools of rock-crystal quartz. There was no such quartz for twenty miles around, and it was far harder to work, yet they did it. Why? Well, with the briefest glance you can decide that the transparent rock-crystal tools were more beautiful: they gleam.

The two adventures into the area of beauty may be easily dismissed by the skeptic as subjective present-day judgment. But I must insist quite objectively that neither the cultural advance in Africa nor that in China had functional necessity; that both were made at economic cost, work, whether of execution or obtaining materials; that both represented a qualitative advance far beyond the day-to-day necessity of our lives. Later art was a direct expression of our hunting way that can most easily be established—as we shall see— with the great Magdalenian paintings of Cro-Magnon time. This recent art was produced by human beings no different from ourselves. What I concern myself with here are those glimpses of beauty and modes of satisfaction that we enjoyed hundreds of thousand of years before the advent of the modern brain.

It may be useful to recall once again what this investigation is all about: the question, Why are we human beings and not chimpanzees? And a difference more stunning than all our wars and all our violence has been our pursuit of that most impractical of qualities, beauty. As I have suggested, an investigation of this sort resembles more a detective story than a normal scientific work. The detective starts out with a most visible reality; a dead man sprawled on somebody's floor. Who did it? And Why? He searches for clues. We start out with a visible reality, the human being, whom we know through introspection, through a lifetime of experience with others, through our accumulated history of a few millennia. And on a profile of that reality has been stamped our impractical pursuit of beauty, whether a pot of geraniums in a kitchen window, the adornments we have hung on our bodies, or the immortal legacies of a Mozart. Why?

Like the detective, we search for clues. Some of our clues, or evidence, may be shakier than others. But then again, two may dovetail, reinforcing each other. As any reader of crime fiction or the daily newspaper must know, timing can be in itself a clue. Two seemingly unrelated events occur at about the same time. Is it coincidence? Or may there be some relationship that we do not understand? In the evolving history of the cultural animal we come on such a coincidence. About 500,000 years ago our African ancestors, with patient skill, brought to perfection the Acheulian hand ax with all its unnecessary symmetry and grace. Also, about five hundred thousand years ago, there were those of us who under most unencouraging conditions began our wanderings about the endless Eurasian space. Why? Why not sooner, or later?

Art is an adventure. When it ceases to be an adventure, it ceases to be art. Not all of us pursue the inaccessible landscapes of the twelve-tone scale, just as not all of us strive for inaccessible mountain-tops, or glory in storms at sea. But the human incidence is there. Could it be that these two impractical pursuits—of beauty and of adventure's embrace—are simply two differing profiles of the same uniquely human reality?

I have deferred until this moment a brief discussion of one of ethology's explorations: exploratory behavior itself. It would be difficult to write a book about it, so little is the literature thus far gathered by the sciences. Yet I do not know an ethologist who would not testify to its reality, varying widely among species. And while one may think of it as closely related to curiosity, still there is more than a shade of difference.

Exploratory behavior is an inner-directed drive to explore the strange, even at a degree of risk to personal survival. Despite the risk, the selective advantages of the exploratory urge are many-sided. New sources of food may be discovered, or new and safer hiding places. Sources of danger, like the smell of a nearby predator, may come your way; or if you are a predator yourself, then the unexpected presence of trackable prey. In a time of environmental change such as drought, past experience accumulated by exploration may guide you to more amiable environments. Afflicted by a population increase of uncomfortable proportions, the stay-at-homes must suffer, while those with stronger exploratory endowment will migrate out of the affected area. Exploratory behavior resembles a broad animal insurance policy in which the investment of a small risk today may equip you with higher survival probabilities tomorrow.

The reverse, of course, can be true, particularly when the animal's enemy is man. Wild ducks are notoriously curious about anything strange, so much so that in Holland and England a traditional trap uses a trained, strangely behaving dog to lure ducks to their fate. Fraser Darling records that poachers, making a strange squeaking sound with the backs of their hands, can entice a hare within slingshot range. The same sound draws a weasel. In the natural world, however, advantages lie all with exploration.

The short-tailed vole will investigate any new object on his territory despite the risk of drawing the hawk's attention. The value of chance-taking has been experimentally demonstrated by L. H. Metzgar, using owls and mice. Those resident mice who have explored their territory thoroughly have a 5 to 1 better chance of survival than transients lacking such education. Starfish will explore a strange place, though they have no proper brain at all. J. Lee Kavanau, in an elaborate experiment which I have described in detail elsewhere, showed that wild-caught white-footed mice, confronted by a maze with 1,205 turns and 445 blind alleys, can without any Skinnerian reinforcements of reward or punishment learn the maze both forward and backward in two or three days. It was exploration for exploration's sake.

Many an authority, like W. H. Thorpe, has related the innate urge to explore to consequent learning. Washburn, commenting on primate play, suggests that prolonged youth could have no survival advantage unless an inner drive led to learning. Harry Harlow has presented the fairly radical proposition that most learning is negative—in other words, learning what not to do—and would be meaningless without an innate drive to explore and try. A traditional zoologist, S. A. Barnett, objects that exploration is learned just like everything else. Behaviorists, blessed with few friends in biology, enthusiastically agree. Another zoologist, W. Z. Lidicker, accepts exploratory behavior as most pronounced in the young, so that the spread of a population is carried on by the strongest and healthiest. Japanese observers of their favorite monkey endorse the superior capacities of the young when dealing with new things. Tinbergen reports one-day-old herring-gull chicks avidly exploring the family territory, an activity they could scarcely have learned from their parents. Paul Leyhausen, an authority on domesticated cats, expresses his conviction that a high level of curiosity in young or old must be an innate character in all predators. D. E. Berlyne, an authority on people, expresses his conviction that in higher animals conflicting images defy acceptances of order, demand more information, and that the central nervous system of higher animals demands a certain input to avoid boredom.

Enough is enough, so let's get back to the adventures that we pursued half a million years ago. I have for long been bemused by a central observation that the most playful, the most exploratory, *and* the most destructive of young animals are primates and carnivores. Leave a young monkey in your room, come back an hour later, and see if there is anything left. He will have taken the joint to pieces. Leyhausen has his cats. But watch your dog when he's been away for the day; he returns to his territory and must investigate every last inch and object. In Berlyne's terms, will he find a conflicting image? This is why we have watchdogs. I myself would be the first to object that these are domesticated species, perhaps bred for certain qualities. Yet when Elisofon and I watched our band of African hunting dogs (zoologically quite unrelated to domestic dogs) with their twenty pups, it was remarkable how adults discriminated between the exploratory propensities of this pup or that. Guarding adults drowsed in the afternoon sun of the sleepy Serengeti plain. Pups played. One might adventure off a bit. Not an adult ear twitched. But there was a certain pup—and because of their quite individual coloring of coat, you could learn which was which—who might begin a bit of adventuring. Then every adult head rose, round ears pressed forward, amber eyes watched. And if, in his explorations of the immense Serengeti, he scampered perhaps fifty yards, then four or five adults would rise, surround him, and bring him back to pup propriety. Oh, Captain Cook, they murmured, and went back to sleep.

What happened in our history, I believe, was a double dose of exploratory behavior. We were primates by inheritance, predators by adaptation. We united the ways of the two most exploratory of animal families. Perhaps in our leaving the forest there were those human Serengeti pups more remarkable than others for susceptibility to adventure's lure. This we cannot know. We know only that we made the leap. And we know only that a day came, about half a million years ago, when we broke loose from the equatorial prison and went out to conquer the world.

Was it all necessity? Was there an increase of population in the tropical world? There is no fossil evidence. Was it an increase of wariness among prey, pressing us on to naïve hunting grounds? But we did not know about the north, so this could hardly have been a cause. Was it because we learned about fire, and so could have moved into hostile climates? But there is no evidence that we learned about the uses of fire until we got there and needed it. Was it because we possessed the superior weapon, the Acheulian hand ax, and so possessed a confidence as hunters in unfamiliar terrain, facing unfamiliar prey? This must have entered into it. Yet in fact these superior weapons, while coming to dominate all western cultures from England to India, did not enter the advance of Pekin man, who got along well indeed without them.

I conclude that the dominant behavior was adventure. It was an urge deeply imbedded in the evolving human being perhaps from the earliest times of the adventurous primate's acceptance of the hazardous hunting way. While we made our slow selective advance of foot and hand, we remained prisoners of our new culture. Even two million years ago, at the early levels of Olduvai Gorge, according to Napier's studies the hand was not yet sufficiently evolved to develop the precision grip necessary for the workmanship of the Acheulian culture. When the time came, we were freed. Size of brain meant little, the social mind meant much. But we were freed of the anatomical limitations that our ape past had placed on our adventuresome inclinations.

All happened slowly. But once freed, the magnet of our nature commanded that we investigate certain blue Ethiopian hills, and what lay beyond. The freedom of our culture said yes, why not? Our anatomy said, Well of course if you want to. And so in the vast concourse of time we moved on past the veto of desert, past the kinds of forest that we had never seen before, into the chill of winters that our equatorial existence had never anticipated, into darkening seasons unknown to a tropical sun, into snowfalls—what were these beautiful, blinding flakes?—into whipping winds that lacerated our skins. But we did not go back. And that is what is so interesting.

Few of us returned to the easy equatorial heartland, despite all adversity. We invented as we went along. We discovered the values of fire and warmth. We designed rude clothing. Sooner or later we experimented with shelter. All were cultural advances without which we would have died in a northern world, just as all had been irrelevant beneath a tropical sun. Undoubtedly there were those of us who returned, or died on the way. But for those of us who pioneered the great world, Pacific to Atlantic, Indian Ocean shores to Arctic desolation, there had to be something more than our sturdy, adapted bodies or our partly adapted two-pint brains. There had to be ancient winds within us, old primate curiosities, newer predator demands for exploration. These were not so much the biological consequences of cultural advance, but very old biological demands—that inhabit us still, to become a dominant quality in the life of our species. Adventure.

If nothing larger can be said about the human being than that we are hedonists—that our lives are exclusively dedicated to the pursuit of pleasure and the avoidance of pain—then what were we doing in Europe in the Ice Age?

The Ice Age

We are guests in a house that does not belong to us. It is a house with a history far longer than our own, somewhat longer than that of life itself. If the house has an owner, then that owner must be regarded as the cosmos. We cannot even look on the sun as our proprietor, for—though it provides us with the light to see by and the shadows that regularly enfold us, the seasons that annually transform our ways, the evaporation of waters and the clemency of rain, the winds that bring us the cool breath of evening or the ruin of hurricanes, though the sun's potent energies provide distinction between the lichen and the ledge it clings to, between the robin and the rock, between life and death—still the sun itself must someday die as all stars die.

Many an ancient people worshiped the sun, were aware of its seeming vagaries, sacrificed a daughter or a stranger to appease it. Many another ancient people, with profound intuition, studied the kingdom of the stars, wondered, and passed on their observations from generation to generation. So today we can know that their curiosities were well founded, since our star is a slight citizen among fellows of its kind, a lonely, unremarkable traveler in space without end. Yet laws of order prevail governing the travels of our sun. We shall never leave our galaxy, our Milky Way, our family of hundreds or billions of fellows. We shall never adventure into true intergalactic space. Nor shall our little sun disobey laws of birth and death that apply to all stars just as they apply to you or to me. And so I must assume that certain vagaries that occasionally afflict our local star reflect inconstancies natural to all stars, even residents of those fugitive galaxies approaching the last red-shift.

This is why I say that the owner of our house, the planet Earth, where we live as temporary guests, must be regarded as the cosmos itself. We are a part of all things. Diligently we study the universe, and we worship an Einstein as once the Aztecs worshiped the sun. Perhaps we do not know why we dedicate our lives and our fortunes to such study; neither did those long-ago peoples who devoted keen eyesight to lifetimes of observation of the visible celestial empire. Perhaps we scorn such simplistic, anthropocentric nonsense as astrology. Yet the endless popular fascination for astrology, a mere half-millennium obsolete, bears its testament that somewhere buried in our unique human way is a recognition that we and the stars are one.

The sciences, with commendable sophistication, dismiss the influence of minor planets on some billions of human beings. You and I as individuals are very small change in the cosmic market place. Not so the sun, from which we derive our life. Servant of larger cosmic forces though our sun may be, we do not for a moment understand, despite all our studies, its vagaries, its inconstancies. Such a vagary was the Pliocene; such an inconstancy was the Pleistocene. And until the sciences can produce excellent evidence of the cause, we must accept each of these remarkable times as an accident.

I have presented the hunting hypothesis for the origin of human uniqueness within the frame of respectable logic based on present evidence. As we move into the Ice Age, I should find it a hypocrisy of surpassing order if I did not emphasize that this logical interpretation, like the logic of a play, would have not the least persuasiveness had it not been for the scenery of Accident. For reasons known only to sun and stars, fifteen million years ago our climate began its slow deterioration. Shall we believe that if the benevolence of climate which existed for an earlier fifty million years had proceeded to the present date, that there would be human beings? I don't. Just as our species has come about as a union between primate intelligence and the carnivorous way, so the human being would be an evolutionary impossibility had it not been for the confrontation of the intelligent primate and a natural accident—the deterioration of climate which after fifteen million years exists with us still.

Yet one cannot conclude that man himself is an accident, any more than the horse. While in times more benign the ape was evolving as a fruit-eater, the horse was evolving as a browser living off the leaves and the buds of ample forests and brush. The little hipparion, whom I have mentioned already, developed the grazing capacity as well. With the Pliocene spread of grasslands, he made his adaptation as we made ours, and all browsing horses became extinct. The horse and man were partners in our capacity to adapt to the most extreme of natural accidents, but our partnership does not imply that our present friendship is of any great antiquity. At a site in France called Solutré, at the foot of a cliff, are the fossil bones of thirty thousand horses. Ice Age man, at one time or another, drove them over the cliffs. The fourth and last ice sheet was all but endless, and only the ruthless survived.

This fourth major wave of glaciation, called in Europe *Würm* and in America *Wisconsin,* contains within it almost the entire history of evolving *Homo sapiens*. One may speak of it as the last glaciation only in the sense that it is the last that we have experienced. We live in an interglacial period, a breathing spell, and glacial times will return. There are many ways of measuring the extent of a glaciation, but the simplest is sea level. How much water has been subtracted from the seas to be locked up in the masses of continental ice? There have been times when our seas have dropped three or four hundred feet the world around. There was that much ice piled up. The last time that we experienced a climate a bit milder than our own, sea levels stood about twenty feet higher than they do today. But this was 120,000 years ago, before the coming of *Homo sapiens*. And coral deposits along the shores of tropical islands indicate that the warm time lasted for little over five thousand years.

It is a chilling thought that in the past half-million years climates as hospitable as our own have prevailed for only about 5 or 10 percent of the time. It is an equally chilling thought, if one turns one's mind to accident, that times like our whole Ice Age have no precedent anywhere on earth in the past 250 million years. And for anyone who follows the sciences with fairly close attention, it is an even more chilling thought how many able specialists are today beginning to worry. But I shall return to the uncertainties of climate in my last chapter.

What we must do here is somehow to identify ourselves with true Neanderthal man as he spread himself about Europe and the Middle East. You and I inhabit and have adapted to a brief time of benevolent climate, and so we take it for granted. Neanderthal, we must assume, took equally for granted the torments of the last glaciation, and he adapted to them magnificently. He had the striking advantage of re-garding such times as normal. So he was a bad-weather ani-mal. We, in a time of little over ten thousand years, have come to regard our benevolent interlude as normal, so we have become good-weather animals. Ours may be no advan-tage at all.

Neanderthal man was first discovered in a German valley, from which he has taken his name, in 1856. A few years earlier, in 1848, his first remains had been found in Gi-braltar but could not be identified. Throughout the early days of Darwinian consequence we regarded him as some bestial link between man and ape. In the textbooks that many of us were raised on, he is a brutal creature with simian face and curved thigh-bones, scarcely able to walk erect. Later discovery, later research rendered all this nonsense. His brain was slightly larger, on the average, than our own. His legs were perfect, though he may have been subject to rickets. Although we long classified him zoologically as a separate species, *Homo neanderthalensis*, today we regard him as a distinct subspecies but nevertheless the first wave of *Homo sapiens*.

Neanderthal appears, quite rarely, in cold but unglaciated times upwards of one hundred thousand years ago. So perfectly do his earliest fossil bones blend with the remains of *Homo erectus*, the Eurasian pioneers, that it becomes anatomically difficult to separate one from the other. Were the 300,000-year-old remains of ancestral man from the Thames Valley, or Hungary, *erectus* or early neanderthaloids, or even very early examples of our own modern breed? It's hard to say. The issue is complicated by an observation that the first neanderthalers—say, from Steinheim in Germany, or from Charente in France, or from Saccopastore in Italy—dating back earlier than the last glaciation, are peculiarly more modern in appearance than the classic Neanderthal of the caveman days of the later vast glaciation.

What is sure is that Neanderthal was a direct descendant of *one branch* of pioneer *erectus*. Bestial he was not, but neither was he good-looking. He had inherited from *erectus* the glowering ridges of bone above his eyes. Like *erectus*, he had a lower jawbone so heavy that you would not have cared to ask him home for a drink; he might have eaten the glass. He was short and he was powerful, far beyond *erectus*. In America when I was young we had a wrestler named Strangler Lewis. In my mind's eye I have always associated Strangler Lewis with Neanderthal. Both were effective.

Neanderthal man was not only effective. In his evolutionary advance from the *erectus* level, he had progressed from the two-pint to the three-pint brain. On the average the Neanderthal brain was a shade larger indeed than our own. And he needed it. The Würm ice sheet that he encountered was not the largest of the Ice Age advances, but it was the longest-lasting and the cruelest. In the course of its grip, nearly seventy thousand years long, there were several brief breathing spells that we call interstadials. None, however, presented weather like ours. They were simply short intervals when times might be described as bad instead of worse. To all these conditions he made his adaptations and survived.

He lacked nothing in the way of game. Nobody, man or animal, could live on the ice itself. But around a wide border lay the tundra that attracted the reindeer just as the Canadian tundra attracts the related caribou today. Farther out might lie patches of pine and birch forest, but mostly it was grassland. What distinguished all was the length and the hardship of the winters, the briefness of the summers. Yet there were those animals other than reindeer and men who made the adaptation—the mammoth and woolly rhinoceros, the cave bear, wolves and foxes, the horse and the powerful aurochs, ancestor to our modern cattle.

The length and severity of Ice Age winters offer another confirmation of the hunting hypothesis. I remind the reader that those authorities who have insisted on the term *hunters-and-gatherers* to describe Pleistocene man, and have concluded from observations of modern hunting peoples that in fact we were largely dependent on plant food, have overlooked the quite simple proposition that in Ice Age Europe and Asia, throughout most of the year, there wasn't any. Except for short interglacial periods of warmth, summers as we know them did not exist. When they came, we unquestionably enjoyed the greens and fast-ripening berries as a welcome change, but even the kind of trees that produce fruit and nuts were absent from the sparse forests of glacial Eurasia. The appearance of hazel is one of the signals marking the retreat of an ice sheet.

From the time of the earliest advent of African-evolved *erectus* in cold Eurasia (Heidelberg man, over 500,000 years ago, is a possible example), we had to be preadapted to a diet consisting exclusively of meat, and equipped with skills of the chase that could guarantee survival. Our African experience, as I have presented it, shows ample evidence. The Ice Age winters presented the test. If the anthropologist is to examine modern hunting peoples, then he must look to those, such as in northern Canada, who live under ecologically comparable conditions. The Copper Eskimo, the Chippewan, the Kutchin, the Kaska include in their diet plant foods ranging from 10 percent to zero.

As part of his adaptation, Neanderthal introduced that sheltered home, the cave. In the Ukraine, where there are many Neanderthal sites, he went further. Using mammoth bones and reindeer skins, he made permanent constructions somewhat resembling the North American tepee, but even more closely the hogan of the Navajo. There must have been earlier structures, such as those found at Nice, just as there were earlier uses of caves like that of *erectus* at Choukuotien. But in western Europe Neanderthal made an institution of the cave. What we mean when we think of home—its shelter, its security, its warmth, its social ties—had its roots in the winters of Würm.

Fire was used by most Neanderthalers, but not all. And so the question whether they knew how to make it must remain open. Hearths are a commonplace in the caves of western Europe, as they are in the mammoth-bone structures of the Ukraine, yet in his excavation of the High Cave at Tangier, Carleton Coon found no evidence for fire. Signs are similarly lacking in most early sites in the Middle East. Coon has made the reasonable suggestion that its principal use was for warmth, so that in regions less pressed by glacial winters, including all of Africa, one could survive without it. Yet in France, at Charente, of two nearby Neanderthal grottoes the one has hearths, the other has not, and they are of the same age. Perhaps the Neanderthals had learned the making of fire, but the technique was so difficult that only some groups boasted fire-masters. It would make sense in terms of the later history of fire-making; but we don't know.

Certainly cooking, as I suggested much earlier, was no part of their culture. Burned bones occur frequently, but if fossilization preserved hackberries for a quarter of a million years in China, then it would have preserved such plant ingredients as roots, and one finds not a trace. What little we know of his feces confirms it. Neanderthal failed to go forward along this cultural line, and along another line he went backward.

At the few very early, preglacial Neanderthal sites we occasionally find the final traces of the Acheulian culture, with the remarkable hand ax which I have described as unnecessarily beautiful. After the full definitive advance of Würm, however, 75,000 years ago, the Acheulian vanished. Perhaps Neanderthal was too busy staying alive to waste his time on fine stonework. The culture known as Mousterian replaced it and is everywhere in Europe associated with Neanderthal man. Mousterian stone tools and weapons to our eyes are cruder. While I cannot here get carried away with details, the technique is that of a flake culture in which from a nodule of flint by a skillful stroke a flake is knocked off. The edges are quite sharp and may be trimmed finer. You may forget about beauty. Neanderthal was a pragmatist.

I find something quite remarkable in an advance of brain size of such order combined with aesthetic retrogression. There is no evidence anywhere in the Mousterian culture of personal adornment or the rudest experiments with art, nor can one seriously explain it by the rigors of existence, since there were the long winter nights, the sheltering cave, and even the dim light of inadequate fires. Again one must recall that size of brain by no means determines everything. In one area, however, there was an advance of significance to all of the human future: Neanderthal began to wonder about death.

In western Europe, occasionally at least, he buried his dead. There seems no customary procedure prevailing in the burials, though skeletons have been found in such a contorted fetal position as to suggest that the corpse was bound tightly. Nor can one read into these burials a concern with an after-life; that would come later with Cro-Magnon. What is conclusive in the advance is that in these close, cave-based social groups, death was impressive and frequent.

Henri Vallois of the Musée de l'Homme in Paris once made a painstaking study of all available Pleistocene skeletal remains and found that women died younger than men, usually before thirty. Very few men passed forty. About half of the Neanderthals died before maturity, almost 40 percent before puberty. He calculated that by the time an individual reached twenty, his mother was almost surely dead, his father near the end. The contact between generations was brief. Death was a quality in abundant supply.

There was an ugly side to the concern for death among one's family and friends, since it implied an appreciation for the value of death in others. Neanderthal did not invent murder and cannibalism, though he practiced them. Purposeful killing goes far back into the australopithecine record. The famous *Homo habilis* of two million years ago apparently died of a blow on the top of his head. When we come down to *erectus* and the caves of Choukuotien, we find the remains of forty individuals. Almost all are cranial bones. There is scarcely a body-bone. The heads had been brought back from somewhere else. I do not know of a competent authority who disagrees with the great student of Pekin man

163

Franz Weidenreich that they were head-hunters and cannibals. From one area of the skull there is not a fragment in the deposit. This is the area at the base that surrounds the foramen magnum, the opening through which the spinal cord connects with the brain. The skulls had been opened to extract the brain, with precisely the same technique that head-hunters in Borneo and New Guinea use today.

Aside from the weapon itself, there is no element in human culture that has persisted so changelessly for so long. Italy's foremost anthropologist, the late Alberto Blanc, found deep in a cave on his own estate at Monte Circeo, less than a hundred miles south of Rome, one of the most famous of Neanderthal skulls. The individual had been killed by a blow on the head, then the foramen magnum opened in a perfect duplicate of the surgery at Choukuotien. Significantly, the skull was surrounded by a little ring of stones. Ritual had entered into the transaction, and there is a general acceptance that ritual murder characterized the extraction and eating of a victim's brain.

The Circeo skull is about 55,000 years old. But far earlier, before the Würm ice sheet, there is the Ehringsdorf skull of a pioneer Neanderthal with the same mutilation. Still earlier, perhaps 200,000 years ago, one finds the remains of a transitional being difficult to classify as *erectus* or Neanderthal. This is the Steinheim skull, carrying the same mark. Nor was the custom confined to Europe. Later Solo man, from Java, left behind the remains of eleven individuals, testifying to some kind of massacre. All had had their brains extracted.

We may speculate about, though we do not understand, the persistent ritual value of eating somebody else's brain. What seems evident, however, is that the value of inflicting death on others long preceded Neanderthal's concern with death as such. He was in no position, of course, to extend his

164

wonderings about the death of family and friends to the mystery of his sudden death as a people.

About 35,000 years ago there was an interstadial, one of those brief fluctuations in which the ice sheet retreated a bit, as if to gather its forces for the later and more savage onslaught which we know as Main Würm. Perhaps for a few thousand years winters were more tolerable, valleys opened up a bit, and migrations became possible. It was in this time that *Homo sapiens sapiens*—ourselves—appeared in western Europe. We loosely call our Ice Age breed Cro-Magnon man. He resembled Neanderthal in neither his anatomy nor his culture.

Gone were the bony masses above the eyes and—significantly—the heavy, sloping jaw. He was tall, strong, differing in no way from a good-looking man of our time. His stone industry, traditionally called *Aurignacian* where earliest we find it, was based mostly on narrow stone blades carefully chipped, probably with hammer and punch. They bear small resemblance to Neanderthal's clumsy flakes. Some were points, seemingly for spears. But he worked with bone and antler and ivory from the mammoth, carving them as Neanderthal never had done. And he cared about art. From one of his earliest sites, about thirty thousand years old, we have the world-famous figurine of a heavily pregnant woman, the Venus of Willendorf. We know so much about Cro-Magnon —yet we do not even know where he came from.

Nor do we know what happened to Neanderthal. A common date for the last Mousterian sites is 35,000 years ago, and you will find such sites in Israel, Gibraltar, France, and Germany. The earliest known Aurignacian site in France, at Abri Pataud in the Dordogne valley, is dated with considerable accuracy at 32,300 years. And you will not find a later Mousterian site or a trace of Neanderthal man in all of Europe or the Middle East.

What happened to Neanderthal is a mystery that has haunted anthropology for many decades. I have heard such imaginative suggestions as that he took one look at Cro-Magnon and got so discouraged that he dropped dead. A favorite idea at one time was that he retreated north with the ice to father the Eskimo. It is anatomically impossible; besides, the ice did not retreat until over twenty thousand years later. There are still authorities who cling to the notion that *sapiens sapiens* is descended from *sapiens neanderthalensis*. It is an easy notion, and that is all. There is one cave in Israel, near Mount Carmel, where the fossil remains could indicate interbreeding. There is no other known example. And besides that there is an evolutionary barricade known as the chin. Neanderthal had none. I discussed this structural advance in *African Genesis* but to the boredom of regular readers I must summarize it here within a different critical context.

From the very earliest time of our separation from the ape and the dependence on our hands and our reduction of fighting teeth, our face began to shorten. No longer did we have to possess power of jaw to reinforce fighting or carrying. But with the shortening of our lower jaw came an anatomical problem. Inspect the jaw of the dog or, if you have one handy, the fox or lemur, and you will find a long slim V, perfect in terms of strong engineering. But with every step of our way along an evolutionary course that accepted no survival value in strong jaws, and at the same time as the increasing brain developed more and more a flattened face, an engineering problem developed with the jaw. We sacrificed the architecture of the V. The chimp not only retained some of the V with his partial snout, but retained also a reinforcing cross-tie known as the simian shelf. Our line did not. So as we progressed through the stage of *Homo erectus,* we had no choice but to reinforce with heavier and heavier bone the lower jaw. That is why I have emphasized its incidence in *erectus* and Neanderthal.

166

With Cro-Magnon, and all races of modern man, came a selective advance of dramatic order. The chin is a flying buttress of sorts which, with its bony projection forward, ties together the linking members of the jaw. The increasing heaviness of bone was no longer necessary. With this inconspicuous anatomical accessory the heavy jawbone became obsolete, the vertical profile of the modern face a probability. Handling fossils, no amateur can overlook the difference that came about in western Europe concerning the appearance of man.

Many conclusions may be drawn from the advent of the chin. It was not even logical, but simply happened to some descendant of *erectus*. And since the improbable chin is a character of all modern races, and remains too unlikely an anatomical adventure to have happened more than once, one must conclude that modern races separated *after* the chin became a fixture. We the Caucasians appeared in western Europe about 35,000 years ago. We were probably just one wave of modern *sapiens sapiens* proceeding, in a climatic breathing spell, towards various ends of the Old World.

In Europe we encountered Neanderthal. We were so unlike him, both in culture and anatomy, that we could not have descended from him. The origin of *sapiens sapiens* is as vexing a question as exists in anthropology. In Hungary one finds our characteristic deposits some thousands of years earlier than in western Europe, and the hint is broad that we came from the East. There is a possible early appearance in Israel. Perhaps—though only just perhaps—the hint is confirmed by the historic tradition of wave after wave of implacable invaders—Huns, Vandals, Magyars, Turks—who far later sprang out of the immensity of the Eurasian steppes. Where we came from, however, must remain a mystery bequeathed to future anthropologists. What happened to Neanderthal, I find no mystery at all.

We killed him off.

No people can vanish in an evolutionary instant through

discouragement, hybridization, flight and migration, encounter with strange diseases, or losing competition with a better-adapted sort. Neanderthal had survived for tens upon tens of thousands of years every hardship that a paroxysm of nature could throw at him. What he could not survive was us.

If a mystery surrounds the disappearance of Neanderthal, then the mystery exists only in the minds of modern humanists, who would prefer not to take the blame. For there is no mystery. By means of a brain with superior organization, perhaps even with superior capacities for speech—by means of superior weapons, superior imaginations, a demonstrably superior culture—we annihilated Neanderthal man. He too had been no gentle being, with his records of mayhem and massacre. At Krapina, near Zagreb, is a rock shelter with over five hundred Neanderthal bones, many showing scars where meat had been cut off. He had not only massacred fellow Neanderthalers but eaten them as well. But when he met us, the strangers, he met a different kind.

There is an obvious objection to my suggestion, Why do we not find similar grim fossil monuments to our encounter? But the English geologist W. W. Bishop, in discussing fossils, once came up with the evocative phrases "environments for life" and "environments for death." He was explaining why you find fossils at one location but not another. In Africa there are the living sites, or the lakesides; in Europe, caves. In such environments for death, remains are most likely to be preserved. But in western Europe we intruders would have encountered Neanderthal on the open hunting grounds where fossil preservation would have been least likely. That we did not look alike would have encouraged animosity, even as it does between peoples today. Above all, we were hunting competitors. Still dependent on the cooperating hunting band for survival, Neanderthal need have lost but a few adult males from his band for the dependent society to be doomed.

In his Serengeti studies George Schaller shows that any predator taking his prey is cool, calculating, methodical. It is a kind of aggressive behavior radically unlike his defense of a kill against competitors. Then there is overwhelming emotion, rage, and sometimes a lethal outcome unlike normal relations within a species. Such would have been the situation between competing hunters in glacial Europe.

Much debate has gone into the origin of the human being's unique disposition to kill his own kind. The charge has sometimes been directed at Konrad Lorenz and me that we attribute human warfare to our animal ancestry, that "war is in our genes." One must charitably assume that the charge has been supported by cocktail party gossip, not by reading our works. Any student of ethology must know that while animals under extraordinary circumstances will kill their own kind, still, in all the vertebrate world, there exists no precedent for the purposeful, massive, organized killing and destruction so tempting to man. And the question that Lorenz and I have asked again and again is, Why are people so different? What went wrong with men?

We have had varying ideas. Lorenz has proposed that with the brain's expansion of the neocortex, certain innate mechanisms inhibiting lethal aggression were lost. I find the proposal quite reasonable, so long as like animal quarrels our differences were personal. But it does not explain our historical record for widespread, systematic violence.

In *African Genesis* I explored another idea, that of man's continual dependence on the weapon for survival which, as we have seen in this narrative, became virtually a portion of his biological equipment. As hunters we were dangerous animals, led necessarily violent lives, and suffered natural selection against those individuals who failed to delight in the chase and the kill. If today we delight in violent action, as all departments of entertainment can testify, the legacy seems a normal one. But again, the organized warfare of men against men fails of explanation.

169

Still searching, I put forward in *The Social Contract* still another hypothesis: that with domestication, the hunting way—which had been the only way we had ever known—turned from the hunting of animals to that most dangerous of prey, man. The proposition seemed so reasonable that it encountered small resistance. Yet I neglected a striking bit of evidence. In 6500 B.C. the agricultural revolution was only beginning to get underway. Even so, the citizens of Jericho, the world's oldest town, were erecting their *third* set of walls. So extensive were the fortifications that they included a ditch outside the walls resembling somewhat a dry moat. The ditch was twenty-eight feet wide, eight feet deep, and carved out of solid limestone. The famous walls of Jericho, demanding such effort, could have been built only by a people long accustomed to the threat of organized attack. But the date was far too early for the threat to have come from idled hunters.

Warfare, at least in this situation, had preceded our fields and our flocks. I cannot believe that such warfare could have been common in our hunting days, when the taking of a slave meant just another mouth to feed, and the conquest of land merely the extension of a hunting range beyond our means to exploit. Yet genocide was another matter. And that is why I have come to believe that massive, systematic destruction of one people by another began with Cro-Magnon's invasion of Europe.

It is a bitter conclusion, though we Caucasians of western Europe need not, in our contemporary fashion, wallow in exclusive guilt for everything. The same process must have taken place wherever the races of modern *sapiens sapiens,* spreading about the Old World, encountered peoples anatomically more primitive than themselves. Had it not been true, then residual pockets of earlier men would have existed into historic times. And it is not so. When our kind of man arrived on the scene, he enforced a human monopoly the world around.

The ghost of Neanderthal haunted me through several seasons. I have described the two subspecies of *Homo sapiens* as probably descended from differing populations of *Homo erectus,* and I have described the pre-Würm Neanderthalers as far more modern in appearance than the later, "classic" Neanderthal man. The coarsening of features and increasing heaviness of bone may have been a response to the rigorous environment of glaciated Europe. Also, I have mentioned that Neanderthal's brain was a shade larger than our own, but its proportions were quite different. What had happened to us was a great increase in the frontal lobe, giving us the high forehead and near-vertical facial profile. His forehead sloped, and the bulk of his brain was at the back in what is sometimes called the "Neanderthal bun." Certainly in the eyes of invading Cro-Magnon he looked different. And how peoples differ—in skin color, stature, facial structure, quality of hair—has been the inspiration for many a cruelty in the history of human conflict.

I was still, however, dissatisfied with my reflections. But then came a stunning contribution from an unexpected field of speculation. In late 1972, less than a year before he died, Louis Leakey and I conducted a public dialogue at the California Institute of Technology concerning the origins of war. (The dialogue was published the following year in *Psychology Today.*) We agreed immediately, from quite different lines of reasoning, that while quarrels may have flourished at an earlier date, war as we know it was impossible until some time later than forty thousand years ago. My evidence was concerned largely with the development of weapons. While it was of interest, it was routine as compared with Leakey's approach.

What seemed significant to me was that before that date we were dependent, so far as we know, on hand-held weapons, thrown stones, and perhaps shaped missiles. We possessed no effective offensive weapon for concerted attack on the part of a large organized group. Not very much later, however, when the Sahara was still a green hunting ground, the bow and arrow was invented by a North African people with a culture known as *Aterian*. The essential invention was the "tanged" point. The much later arrowhead of the American Indian is an example. By means of an indentation near the base, stone points could be neatly hafted—small points to arrows, large points to throwing spears. It became possible to kill at a distance without the close-quarters danger of the hand-held weapon.

Surprisingly, the bow and arrow spread very slowly. Perhaps the early bows were weak. Perhaps the last, vast surge of the Würm glacier, preventing migration, discouraged its spread into Europe. We know that it never reached Cro-Magnon. And until a very late date, its spread to the east was blocked by mideastern devotion to the sling. The story of David and Goliath has its background of fact, for the Hebrews were among those who perfected the sling's accuracy. Even Alexander the Great, in his eastern conquests, encountered warriors whose proficiency with the sling exceeded that of his own Greek archers. Perhaps it was this mideastern indifference to the bow and arrow that blocked its spread farther into Asia, which would explain why the weapon did not reach the American Indian until less than two thousand years ago.

Nevertheless, or so it seemed to me, it was the idea of the long-distance weapon, whether bow and arrow or sling or thrown spear, inflicting maximum damage with minimum risk, that made possible organized warfare. My argument, as I say, I regard as routine. Leakey's, which concerned speech and fire and night life, was spectacular.

Our agreement on the date of more or less forty thousand years rested on the coincidence that this also was the date for the universal appearance of fire-making. (He agreed, on African evidence, with my estimate.) But Leakey's grand imaginative leap was that the institution of fire meant the invention of night life. Before that, like birds or baboons, with the fall of darkness we sought our perch. Our daytime lives were pragmatic, absorbed with the chores of survival. The leisure of the evening was for the human being like a new ecological niche. There was the security of the shelter or cave, and the social focus of the fire that fascinates us yet today. Now talk became a pleasure, not a necessity. The day's adventure of the hunt could be told and retold, while children listened and learned. Memories were enhanced, myths began to take form. The skilled story-teller emerged with his gifts for imagination, symbols, abstract concepts. And perhaps the first concepts to emerge were *us,* to describe the fireside group, and *them,* meaning everybody else. So deep is its grip that the concept endangers us yet.

But as Leakey the skilled story-teller related it, there came also such concepts as good and evil, good guys, bad guys, friends, enemies, and reward and revenge. Not until such concepts became a commonplace in our thinking could we perpetuate our hatreds, organize our animosities. Not until such concepts became the property, not just of isolated bands, but of the mosaic of bands that we think of as the tribe, could there be the common appeal, the common invocation of emotions, the common jargon that makes organized warfare possible.

Not our animal inheritance but our most priceless, uniquely human endowment, the capacity to communicate abstract symbols, has been responsible for warfare.

The capacity for conceptual thought must have an earlier evolutionary basis. In the hands of *erectus* the achievement of the Acheulian hand ax was a creation guided not by his materials but by a concept in the mind of the artisan. Head-hunting and the eating of brains may be accepted as superstition with magical expectations; but these very expectations speak of a concept. I, more than did Leakey, believe that a human type of speech must have taken form in fairly early hunting days, even possibly australopithecine. Leakey is correct that hunting is a silent occupation, and Schaller is correct that lions need no speech to coordinate their cooperative hunts. But the surprising capacity of chimpanzees for vocabulary and syntax, and the selective pressure that must have been exerted on our hunting societies for better communication between male and female, and between adults and slow-growing young, could only have encouraged a speech more definitive than animal communication. The social mind demanded maximum accuracy of even rudimentary speech.

Noam Chomsky seems to be winning his argument that the learning of language has a biological foundation. My hunting hypothesis must naturally second his argument. But there is an abyss between the chimp capacity for *give me* and *me give,* which may have been ours for the last three million years or more, and the symbolized abstractions that Leakey has emphasized. Somewhere along the line of *sapiens* evolution came an independent development of complex conceptual capacity in the *sapiens sapiens* line. I have discussed the greater development of the brain's frontal lobe in our subspecies. The lobe contains the speech centers. Perhaps in our line, for reasons yet unknown to science, there was a greater selective advantage for neural circuitry which eased the learning and expansion of language. We are speculating. But perhaps Neanderthal bands in mountainous, glacial Europe lived a life far more isolated, with far less need for larger communication, than did our own ancestors—where? on the eastern steppes?

We do not know. What we do know is that the capacity for speech must have preceded our capacity for communicated conceptual thought. The hunting way must, through natural selection, have encouraged our capacity for speech.

174

And what we are considering is the Leakey thesis that this capacity for speech, with the advent of fire, opened up the new human opportunity for myths and discussion, concepts of friendship and animosity, them and us, the organized enmities that could lead to war.

The advent of communicable concepts, whether in speech or thought, led to avenues more amiable than warfare. There was a further advance in the story of cooperative hunting. Now bands got together in communal hunts, leaving stacks of mammoth bones as a monument. Driving animals as nimble as horses over the cliff at Solutré could have been accomplished only by a large number of hunters. Neanderthal left no such record. And then there was art.

In calling all of these modern peoples *Cro-Magnon* I have, as I have said, used the term loosely. There were probably several waves of people who entered Europe through valleys between the glaciated Alps and the Carpathian Mountains. Physically indistinguishable, they may have brought varying cultural traditions to the West before Main Würm froze up the continent and ended migration. To follow all of these traditions, such as Aurignacian, Gravettian, Solutrean, is too complex for any but a specialized study. And so, following common usage, I have used the term *Cro-Magnon man* to apply to all of the wave of modern beings, although in a strict sense it should be applied only to the authors of the Magdalenian culture which, at the climax of the Ice Age, presented us with the eternal magnificence of the great cave paintings, acknowledged by all as our first true art.

Yet from his first appearance, in such contrast to Neanderthal, art was the most visible illumination of the Cro-Magnon way. I have described the Acheulian hand ax as beautiful beyond need. The Solutreans produced, by the same technique of pressure-flaking, spearheads so beautiful as to be useless. So perfect is the symmetry, so delicate the flaking—and above all, so thin is the finished blade—that had they been used they would have snapped in two. Perhaps the authors got carried away by art for art's sake. Or perhaps they were intended for rituals.

Or one may turn to a site as far from France as Sungir, a bit north of Moscow, where three skeletons of the time have been found with strings of beads clinging to them. There is every indication that they had been sewn to fairly close-fitting clothing. It seems reasonable, since everywhere one finds needles, with eyes, made from bone. Figurines, usually of women, are common both in the Ukraine and in Russia proper. Richard Klein, our authority on the little-known discoveries in the Soviet Union, suggests that beyond the artistic bent of our kind, our adaptation to glacial conditions was superior to that of Neanderthal. Busy Russian archaeologists have never found a Mousterian site north of the latitude of Moscow. But Ice Age sites of our kind (to describe them as Cro-Magnon seems a bit far-fetched) have been found as far north as the Arctic Circle. It is unfortunate that the Russians, excellent and dedicated archaeologists, can turn to so few laboratories for absolute dating. Perhaps it is time for a bit of carbon-14 détente, since for all we know the primal grounds for the evolution of *sapiens sapiens* may lie within the area of the Soviet Union.

Objects of art and adornment—not only figurines but beads, pierced shells, carved bone and ivory—dot the map of late Ice-Age Russia, just as they do the map of southern Europe. All were as much a consequence of conceptual thought—which must lean on language and symbols—as organized social cooperation or social antagonisms.

Only in France and Spain, however, did we ever accomplish the triumphs of Magdalenian cave painting. Our preoccupation with art was with us from the time we first invaded the West and, in my opinion, annihilated Neanderthal. Delivery of death and delivery of beauty came hand in hand. We made our early engravings on antler or bone, later

176

on cave walls. We added a single color, like ocher, as time went on. Then at last came the burst of polychromatic painting—almost always of animals—that made Cro-Magnon famous. It was fortunate for me that I visited the Dordogne Valley's great cave, Lascaux, in 1955, before the humidity of tourists so threatened the paintings with ruin that French intervention closed the cave. It was an experience that one is unlikely ever to forget. Surrounded on walls and roof by animals of grace and bulging power, one could only conclude that if the human being, in the last depths of the Ice Age, could produce such artists, then someday we should produce our Michelangelo.

But why did we do it? Almost all authorities agree, I believe, that ritual guided our hands—the rituals of a hunting people that would lend hope to the hunt and protection for the hunter. The charging bulls of Lascaux speak of terror and death. It may be useful to recall the life expectancy of Neanderthal; for all our superior capacities, the expectations of Cro-Magnon were no better.

And that is why I have come to believe that the central concept that we brought to evolving man was the concept of death. Neanderthal may have wondered about it, and like his predecessors found virtue in sacrificing a stranger and eating his brains. Cro-Magnon, so far as I know, never practiced the ancient cannibalistic custom. But from early days he painted his dead with red ocher. While there may be other explanations, I find it difficult myself to believe that his thoughts about death did not include hopes for immortality. The association of the color of blood with life everlasting finds little expression today beyond the red shroud that envelopes a dead pope. Yet as late as classic times it was common, and Homer recalls the red shrouds of dead heroes.

Burial of the dead is in itself a mark of respect for the dead. Neanderthal practiced it occasionally, Cro-Magnon commonly and with considerable evidence of ceremony. The skeletons from the vicinity of Moscow, still with the beads on their clothing, come from a burial site. Carved ornaments of shell and teeth are frequent companions, though I am aware of no evidence for the burial of tools or weapons for use in the after-life. Odd bits of magic appear, though, such as the inconspicuous canine teeth of the deer. According to Blanc, it is still the trophy most favored by hunters in central Europe.

Magic was everywhere. There is a bison engraved on a cave floor at Ariège with three spear-points in its side. As Oakley has written, it differs little from such a contemporary superstition as sticking pins in the wax image of an enemy. At another site near Ariège is the wall painting of the famous "sorcerer," half-human, half-animal. Perhaps it is a shaman involved with the ritual, or perhaps it is a mythic figure representing a god of the animals. Many a frieze of bison or horse, though seemingly decorative, is far more likely to commemorate a totemic belief.

The mystery and the darkness surrounding cave art is impressive to me. Although the chambers of Lascaux are reasonably accessible, there are other caves where you must proceed perhaps two hundred yards into the earth's blackness before, with an electric torch, you find an engraved or painted wall. Before we had the light of fire, such work was of course impossible. But why, with our primitive torches, did we purposely choose such inaccessible places? Was it the mystery of dark places that enhanced the magic of the shrine?

Death was our constant companion in the last crushing grasp of the Ice Age. Death awaited us at every unexpected corner—awaited the child, the mother, the hunting father out on crumbling slopes or featureless tundra. Art was our instrument for mastering death, as death was our instrument for mastering others.

Interglacial Man

In the autumn Old Lyme, Connecticut, snuggles down beneath its towering maples, its beeches, its black-limbed ashes of such symmetry that one might think that the author was contemplating the structure of a Greek vase. The cold winds blow; the leaves come down. You trudge knee-deep in the scarlet, golden, purple, silver harvest of leaves. When you have wearied of New York's geometry and glassy arrogance, then it is where you would like to be. Yet near Old Lyme is Rogers Lake, an inconspicuous adornment among the woods and the fields, and beneath the lake is an ordered layer-cake of sediments reaching back into the last glaciation. Each layer has preserved with impartial authority the pollen of its period—the imperishable record of what grew where and when—so that with small doubt one may visualize landscape after landscape of times gone past. There isn't too much difference for the last ten thousand years. But go back fifteen thousand, and you will find pollen scarce, consisting almost entirely of sedges and grass, along with an occasional pine. Connecticut was tundra.

Go back the same fifteen thousand years to an unglaciated area beside the frozen Arctic near Point Barrow, Alaska. The landscape differs scarcely at all: the same sedges, the same grasses, a few dwarf willows, so say the preserved pollen. The artist's Connecticut paradise has changed much since those days; Point Barrow little.

Scan the earth of fifteen thousand years ago. It was the

time when in the Spanish Pyrenees and France's Dordogne Valley, Cro-Magnon hunters, painting their immortal bulls and deer and horses deep on the walls of caves, reached the climax of their art. The last great ice sheet had likewise just reached its climax. For sixty thousand years it had held us in its inexplicable grip. In North America it reached as far south as the Ohio River and, as recently discovered, even into North Carolina. Chicago stood beneath a crunch of ice well over a mile deep; the calculation is easily made, since the seas were three hundred feet shallower than now, and it would have taken that much onshore ice within the known margins of the glacier to have effected such a subtraction. In Europe the Ukraine, where today January temperatures seldom rise above the freezing point, would on the Fahrenheit scale have been about fifteen degrees colder. How hunters and their families survived with their niggling hearths and their huts of mammoth bones and reindeer skin, I do not know. Nor was the Southern Hemisphere neglected. Glaciers left their records from New Zealand to the Andes. Neither was it a matter of how near the poles you were. Van Zinderen Bakker, a South African pioneer of climate-interpretation through fossil pollen, has given long inspection to the slopes of Mount Kenya, standing directly on the equator. Fifteen thousand years ago the mountainsides were approximately nine degrees Fahrenheit colder than today.

This was our world, and this is how it had been for some sixty thousand years. There had been brief oscillations of climate, as I have already suggested, when the last of the four great ice sheets withdrew a bit, hesitated as if to think things over or renew its resources, then came on again, never relinquishing its sovereignty. During the last of those rugged respites Cro-Magnon entered Europe, and at the time of Lascaux there was no least indication that the eternity of ice and cold would surrender any portion of its jurisdiction. And for two or three thousand more years, it is true, nothing changed. Then something happened. Despite all speculation, all weighty scientific arguments, we do not know what.

The enormous, virtually everlasting Würm ice sheet suddenly faded away. How rapidly it all happened defies belief as it defies explanation. There seems to have been a critical moment about 12,300 years ago. After that came another world, one that evolving *Homo sapiens* had never seen. At Old Lyme, in the course of a very few centuries, pollen shows us that the tundra was gone, forests of spruce and oak were appearing, and vegetation so multiplied that the pollen count in the layer-cake beds increased tenfold. Birch appeared at Point Barrow. Heather was leaping up the slopes of Mount Kenya like an athlete. In Chile the glaciers fled up the Andes valleys.

Throughout all the world, snow melted faster in summer than it could collect in winter. The rushing melt-water gouged new valleys and filled such inland freshwater seas as the Great Lakes. In North America the retreating ice sheet which in its terrifying past had stripped a Labrador down to bedrock, now deposited its rich loam elsewhere to underwrite the soils of the Mississippi Valley.

As the ice vanished, as melt-waters temporarily had to find new courses to the sea, so present dry canyons like the Grand Coulee of the American Northwest were created. But of course it was the ocean itself that felt the immediate effect. It rose, and that is how we can calculate so correctly how much ice lay on the land. We still have the sea-mounts—inundated mountains flattened off by the waves of ages past, now hidden. And it was in this time—before the seas could rise too far to cover the land-bridge between Asia and America, yet just late enough so that that the melting glaciers could uncover a land-route into the Americas—that Paul Martin's skilled hunters crossed over from Siberia. Here in the new continents they would discover species after species innocent of human ways, and these animals would become extinct. The hunters would become the American Indian.

These were turning-point times in the history of evolving man, and what one must observe with awe is how fast they happened. Within a few brief centuries the winds of warmth touched all the earth and everywhere the lives of men. The withdrawal of polar despotism meant that ocean currents took their present ways. Trade winds, monsoons, prevailing westerlies brought their blessings of rain to regions long dry. Not always were they blessings. The Sahara had been green, a hunter's happy land. Now it slowly dried up as the westerlies, long blocked by Arctic dominance, long denied the Gulf Stream's steamy contributions, shifted their damp attention to Europe. Fly low over the Sahara and observe the pattern of water-courses now covered by drifting sand. But look also to Europe, for blessings could be mixed. Within centuries European forests were taking deep root. The tundra and the grasslands were in panic retreat, and with them went the reindeer, the mammoth, the herds of wild horses, almost all of the prey animals that had been our staple throughout all our northern years.

Hunters became an endangered species. Despite its fruits and its nuts, the forest without its grazing species is a poor place to hunt. The last of the Pleistocene hunters, our Cro-Magnon fellows—masters of art and the crafts—presumably followed north along the line of retreat of the tundra and their traditional game, leaving no heirs. Presumably they quietly vanished, and their great art with them.

But how quickly it had all happened! A civilization—and with difficulty one can deny Cro-Magnon the term—vanished. For tens of thousands of years, history had built up to the climax of Lascaux and Altamira. Then in an evolutionary eye-blink, ecological support was withdrawn. The hunting life was ended.

In the uplands of Anatolia and Iraq and Iran new peoples were coming into their own. Wild grasses grew in profusion, the ancestors of wheat and barley. And among the human souvenirs that archaeologists dig up is the sickle, a tool usually made of deer antler with tiny flints imbedded on one side. We were reaping the wild grasses for their seeds, and since by now our use of fire was universal, we were cooking the otherwise indigestible grain. By accident or design—who knows?—we domesticated the wild grains. By nature they had brittle husks that the wind could spread. We selected—by accident or design—the harder-husked mutants that we could handle and sow.

Fields replaced grasslands, grain replaced game. To describe the process as an evolutionary instant is correct in long-term statement, incorrect in our own. I have visited in Israel the kibbutz Sha'ar Hagolan, down in the Jordan Valley near the Sea of Galilee, where the kibbutzniks discovered a neolithic village beneath some ponds, about 8,500 years old. Israelis divide their lives, as is well known, between defending their present and investigating their past. Recoveries from the neolithic village were displayed in an underground bomb-shelter museum. About half were sickles, half weapons of the chase.

We were planting, but we were still hunting. Until recently it was believed that we domesticated animals through the surplus food of our fields, but we now discover that at the great Shanidar cave in northern Iraq, thousands of years earlier, we had converted the wild mouflon into tractable sheep. Sonia Cole, in her definitive *Neolithic Revolution*, records the remarkable evidence. The wild mouflon and domesticated sheep are difficult to distinguish anatomically, but Shanidar goes well back into our hunting past, and its early levels show that about 25 percent of wild kills are under one year old. It is a normal percentage at hunting sites. But then suddenly the percentage of young mouflon jumps to 60 percent. We had manageable flocks and were cropping them at an optimum age. Mouflon were now sheep.

How had we done it? Dogs seem to have been our earliest animal partners, helping in the hunt while enjoying our scraps. We may have trained dogs to protect the sheep from predators. Ethology supports the answer. It was Lorenz who discovered imprinting. Among certain species very young animals, only a day or two old, will attach themselves with a lifelong bond to whatever animal appears first in their lives, regardless of species. Pups and lambs are famous for being imprinted by human beings. Perhaps the very beginnings of domestication amount to no more than the hunter's bringing home wolf-pups or mouflon-lambs as pets for his children, and discovering that he had established an adoption agency.

However animal domestication was accomplished, sheep seem to have been easy. The event at Shanidar was almost eleven thousand years ago, and it would be thousands of years before cattle appeared from Greece to the mideastern highlands. All were descended from the formidable aurochs which we had hunted through the Ice Age. By then, however, we had our fields and the temptation of surplus food to offer. Goats, pigs, and—at a very much later date—horses became our servants. While other areas than the Mideast had less luck with animals, still, fairly soon rice paddies were appearing in Southeast Asia, and maize fields in Mexico.

There is a mystery of sorts why the domestication of plants should have come about in three presumably unrelated areas of the earth at about the same time. The new benevolence of climate may have had something to do with it. The rapid, universal spread of hearths and reliably controlled fire had of course been a necessary premise for dependence on cooking. Or perhaps there was a growing shortage of game. What remains no mystery at all, however, was that the Neolithic Revolution, with its supply of high-calorie foods never known before, was the most overwhelming advance in the history of the cultural animal.

An advance it was, but just like all the others it compelled biological consequences. We have seen how with the use of the weapon our fighting teeth retained no selective value, and so we became dependent on the weapon in the hand. We have seen how our dependence on hunting and meat-eating compelled the adaptation of our feet to the terrestrial life, and so we could never go back to the trees. We have seen how—first with our understanding of the value of fire, then our supreme invention of how to make it—human populations spread to cold regions of the earth where without fire they would perish. And now, with the application of fire and cooking to such plant foods as cereals and legumes, we made available to human nourishment seemingly inexhaustible supplies never before available to the hunter.

The biological consequence, of course, was a population explosion.

It takes from three to seven square miles of hunting range to support one person. Even with the invention of the sling, the shaped spearhead, and the tanged stone-point making possible the bow and arrow, nothing improved the supply of animals. Reliable estimates place the limit of human numbers throughout all the world, ten thousand years ago, at but a few million. Five thousand years later, even though the new way of life had not spread very far, our numbers had probably passed 100 million.

Once again, we could never go back. The hunting life, which had sustained us for such millions of years, was ended. The hunting way, which had molded us, directed our adaptations both anatomical and social, encouraged our skills of tool-making and speech, and lent selective value to a greatly enlarged brain with all its potentialities—which from first to last had determined that we be human beings and not chimpanzees—was gone forever. We could not go back. Now there were too many of us.

As is fairly common knowledge—excepting among contemporary ideologists wielding political axes unblunted by human compassion—the explosion did not stop there. At the opening of the Industrial Revolution there were perhaps 750 million of us. Two centuries later, in 1950, the number was about 2.5 billion. By the end of our century, barring a probable catastrophe, our numbers should have more than doubled. And the probable catastrophe refers not at all to war and weapons. It concerns climate.

Lionel Tiger and Robin Fox, in their *Imperial Animal,* made the iconoclastic observation that our neolithic mastery of food supply may not have been quite the cultural advance that we have always believed. They could be right. Throughout all our hunting years we lived as one species among others—a species of grand endowment and accomplishment, but nevertheless one with its own niche in the natural world of no greater distinction than that of elephant or lion or wolf. With control over fields and herds, we gained a position of privilege possessed by no other vertebrate animal; we became a species apart. No longer were we and all living things partners in an ancient, balanced ecological design. We were masters. And the illusion followed easily that we were masters of nature itself.

The Judeo-Christian religion did little to banish the illusions from the dedications of western man. When on the sixth day of creation God blessed us, and instructed us to be fruitful and multiply, and to go forth and conquer the earth and master all the fish in the seas, all the birds in the heavens, all the animals on the earth, it is a pity we took Him so literally. For what we were given was a free, sanctified, one-way ticket to catastrophe.

Today, with some gloom, we inspect the destination on that ticket. With what élan we went out to master nature, succeeding only in damaging it. With what cheer we founded our faith on our old friend fire, until the day would come when we would be presented with the fuel bill. With what

186

excitement we killed off the wilderness of animals on whom we once depended; with what careless abandon we poisoned the land and the waters and the skies above us. After all, they had been given to us. Dutifully we even obeyed the injunction to be fruitful and multiply.

With some reason one might conclude that nature, in the late twentieth century, is taking her revenge. Yet there is a paradox. When our most severe punishment arrives it will be for no sin of ours, but rather for God's forgetfulness. Carried away, perhaps, by His matchless creation, the Garden of Eden, He forgot to mention that all He was giving us was an interglacial.

On January 26, 1972, a group of able scientists representing many nations and many fields of study held a meeting at Brown University, in Providence, Rhode Island. The report of the meeting was drawn up by two world authorities on climate, George Kukla of the Czech Academy of Science and R. K. Matthews of Brown, and published inconspicuously in *Science* late in the year. The subject was a chilling one indeed: when and how will the present interglacial end?

It is fairly common knowledge that since about 1960 world climate has been deteriorating. Not quite so common is the knowledge that throughout recorded history weather has moved in cycles. Some can be short, like those associated with the eleven-year cycle of sunspots; some, unexplained, can be long and last for a century or two. The Danes fell victim to such a cold cycle about A.D. 1250. The previous centuries had been so mild that they had established their colonies even in Greenland, then aptly named, and pressed on with their explorations of America. But then came the switch. Pack-ice pressing down from the Arctic exerted its veto on navigation. Greenland could no longer be reached, and further exploration of the West was abandoned. Even in England, more than a century later, there stood the remains of abandoned farming villages. We assumed depopulation to be the work of the Black Plague, but it was not. The growing season had become too short.

Another such cycle chilled the northern world beginning about 1600, in the days when William Shakespeare was writing his tragedies. Commonly known as the "Little Ice Age," it too lasted for approximately a century and a half, and competent geologists assure me that the growing season would have been so shortened, in the major wheat-growing regions of Canada and Russia, that crops would have been impossible. In those days, of course, such regions attracted us for their furs, not their wheat.

Fortunately for us, the Little Ice Age had expired by 1750, when the Industrial Revolution inaugurated our present population explosion. We have never experienced one since. Fortunately also for our peace of mind, it would be false to apply to these cycles of cold a simple arithmetical progression, from A.D. 1250 to 1600 to 1950. We know much too little about them. Nevertheless it is legitimate to wonder what would happen to our overcrowded planet if we encountered in the near future a century or two of radically diminished food supply, a time of wildly fluctuating weather marked by unpredictable winters and summers, late springs, early frosts, floods, droughts. Aberrations of the sort seem a character of our interglacial. But what if the sober authorities gathered at Brown University were correct concerning the drastic possibility that we are nearing the end of our interglacial? And that the end will be abrupt?

Even in January, 1972, a significant bit of evidence concerned Baffin Land, Canada's enormous Arctic island half the size of Texas. For thirty or forty years Baffin Land had been free of snow in summer. Now it was permanently snow-covered. It may be useful to recall that a major ice sheet starts most simply when the summer sun fails to melt away the previous winter's snow, so that when autumn comes new snows pile on old. It was the same process, operating in reverse, that 12,000 years ago melted away in a few centuries the ice sheet that had afflicted us for almost 65,000 years. Perhaps the summers were hot, or, with less likelihood, the winters were dry and snowless. In either case, the sun was the winner.

The irony of the Baffin Land report arose from later study of photographs taken by weather satellites. The very winter in which the scientists were meeting would be recorded as the worst in recent history. Permanent snow cover and ice-pack increased by 12 percent throughout all the Northern Hemisphere and failed to melt away the following summer. Difficult to accept though their conclusions may seem, according to the calculations of George and Helena Kukla only six more such winters, coming not too far apart, could restore the Northern Hemisphere to the maximum conditions of the Würm ice sheet, twenty thousand years ago, when Chicago lay mile-deep in ice.

Winters were bad enough in Chicago when I was walking to school, but even so my imagination rejects a future portrait of my native city's slums and skyscrapers ground down beneath the burden of a guest so preposterous. I find a ludicrous quality, as in bad science fiction, and I must presume that my reader does too. But the defect is in our imagination, not nature's. Throughout the length of the Ice Age such a portrait would be normal; from nature's view it is Lake Michigan's sunny shores that speak of bad science fiction.

According to many authorities, including world-famous Caesar Emiliani, in the past half-million years climates comparable to our own have prevailed for only about 10 percent of the time. I have seen estimates as low as 5 percent. We may be quite sure that the last time we experienced weather a shade warmer than today was 124,000 years ago. At about that time the hippopotamus grazed in Britain. At precisely that time in Hawaii, on the island of Oahu, coral beaches were formed seven meters higher than the present sea level. Less water was held back from the seas by glaciers than is today held back by such ice caps as Greenland and Antarctica. Once again I must mention that the level of past seas, together with our new techniques of absolute dating through the regular decay of unstable radiogenic isotopes, reveal to us, for example, the quantity of ice held fast on the continents when at the height of the last glaciation the seas stood a hundred meters lower than now. So it is we may calculate the pleasures of the last heat wave. But what the coral beaches on Oahu and other islands recorded was a phenomenon that did not last long, as I have earlier suggested. Studies from Barbados show that within five thousand years sea levels were dropping rapidly as once again, somewhere, the ice piled up. That happy time, like ours, had been an incident.

A natural accident of climatic charity has been the mother of our civilization. Textbooks, properly reflecting our capacity for self-delusion, may reverently refer to the present era as the *Holocene,* and thus wishfully divorce it from the rambunctious Pleistocene. But any student of the Ice Age knows that the time of the glaciers has not ended. Civilized man, from the time ten thousand years ago when he began his domestication of crops and herds, is as much a child of the Ice Age as was Neanderthal or Cro-Magnon. We have the luck, and that is all, to inhabit a more gracious interval. But we who have recognized our interglacial status have nursed our own comfortable illusions. We have assumed that major glaciations come and go at a slow rate, and that what may happen to us in a few thousand years need not press too sharply on our nerve-ends today. Brown University ruined that assumption.

An ice core bored in the Greenland ice cap showed that ninety thousand years ago there was a drop in temperature, all within a century, that if encountered today would wipe out the major cereal-growing regions of temperate climates, north and south. The kill would have included the entirety of Canada, most of the American Mississippi Valley, virtually all of the Soviet Union, much of China, and the cereal-growing regions of Australia and Argentina.

One may say, "Well, so ninety thousand years ago." But like the warning signal of bird or baboon, it suggested just how fast things can happen, whether in a wilderness of predators and bush or in a wilderness of ice and time. And while there remains a certain excuse for our lack of awareness of the Camp Century ice core, since it has been drilled so recently, still the sophisticated student of the Ice Age should have applied his logic to the hasty retreat of the last great glaciation. If an icy institution as ancient as Würm can vanish in a few centuries, then it is a risky assumption to believe that the next one must accumulate at a pace more deliberate.

But there has been substantial evidence beyond logic, or a single Greenland ice core, to substantiate the rapidity of ancient climate changes. Cold subarctic waters of the north Atlantic have pressed suddenly as far south as Florida, and warmth-loving plankton species have vanished from the Gulf of Mexico. Around Prague and Brno in Czechoslovakia, broadleaf forests have been replaced by grasslands, the grasslands in turn by dust, torrents, and badlands. In Greece interglacial forest has been replaced by grass; in the Netherlands and Denmark, the grass by tundra—and all are phenomena of a very few centuries.

Yet perhaps the most disturbing of the Brown conclusions related to the duration of interglacials. In all the past half-million years there has never been one, with a climate comparable to our own, that has lasted more than ten thousand years. And ours has lasted just over ten thousand years. Studies of early interglacial lake-bed sediments in both England and Germany have revealed not only the same limited duration, but—through pollen analysis—the same inner cyclical variability of climate. Ours has been unique only in that *Homo sapiens* had evolved to inhabit it.

The comfortable idea that if eventually we had to face the worst, then the worst would be a long time coming, vanished at Brown. Optimistically the end of our interglacial might be two thousand years away. By that time we probably would have submitted ourselves to nuclear annihilation, exhausted our natural resources, committed genetic suicide aided by a variety of fashionable social philosophies, so poisoned our environment that life became untenable, so overcrowded it that life became unendurable: a mere ice sheet could represent nothing but novelty to doomsday philosophies and lend, in truth, a certain spice to our less glorious meditations. But what if the crisis came sooner rather than later? Nothing in the Brown University evidence suggested gradual change. The Camp Century ice core in Greenland indicated what could happen in a hundred years; the rapid retreat of the last ice sheet meant quite simply that nature is in charge; and what could happen in two thousand years could happen tomorrow.

The Brown meeting caught little attention. Perhaps its report on the movements of the armadillo fascinated the popular press while turning off responsible authorities. A Nebraska specialist reported that the warmth-loving beast had moved from Mexico into the American Midwest around the turn of the century and was now heading back toward Mexico. For the press it was good fun. For the student of the Ice Age, however, or for an ethologist such as myself, any unscheduled migration of animals is disturbing.

The armadillo made greater sense when new papers began to appear in the scientific journals. One was the Kuklas' report on satellite observation. Another was that of Reid Bryson, director of the Institute of Environmental Research at the University of Wisconsin. In London, *Nature* magazine printed four papers in a single issue. Then the story hit the public press.

Before all the present consternation and controversy about climate began, I had been perturbed by the outcome of the Soviet's virgin land scheme. For a variety of reasons agriculture has been the most spectacular failure in the Russian utopian dream. (The summer following the disastrous winter of the Brown meeting saw the cagy Russians, keeping their crop catastrophe in their ample closet of well-kept secrets, buy up all the loose wheat in the world—a gambit they seem to have repeated more publicly in 1975.) Much earlier, however, when the shrewd peasant Khrushchev became Number 1, he inaugurated the daring scheme of converting thousands of square miles of Siberian lands to grain fields. Admittedly the land was marginal and largely underlain by permafrost. But on the records of the previous half-century the Soviet Union had every reason to suppose that in any ten-year period they would get two crop failures, two fair years, and six bumper crops—a more than ample return. The scheme, into which the Soviet Union poured incalculable resources, could not have encountered worse timing. It matured about 1960 to witness crop failures in 1962, 1963, and many following years, calamities that persist to the present. When that bold and amiable despot suddenly became an unperson in 1964, he was a victim I believe as much of climate as conspiracy.

Bryson's paper demonstrates that the half-century preceding 1960 has had no equal or near-equal, in terms of benevolence, in a thousand years. Even the armadillo got tricked into coming north. Understandably, the Russians presumed that the next half-century would resemble the last and so embarked on their vast scheme. Yet not even the Danes in their time of discovery had weather as warm as ours. Nor, back in A.D. 1250, when the crash came, was there a global problem of feeding 3.5 billion people.

193

One of Bryson's contributions has been to demonstrate what a small change in average annual temperature can do to a crop. A drop of 1 degree Centigrade (1.8 degrees Fahrenheit) shortens the growing season by two weeks. But that is not the full extent of the damage, since the cooler growing-days promote less growth. The actual crop damage is 27 percent. Compensations can be arranged: more land can be planted, more fertilizer applied, hardier crops planted. But let the average temperature drop by 2.4 degrees Centigrade, and the damage will be doubled to 54 percent. For this there can be no compensation, since it is catastrophe.

A political problem of high future order rests on the unhappy truth that the superpower, Russia, with all its ambitions, must count among its resources a large portion of the Arctic Circle. It is a frontier country, standing on the border between the possible and the impossible. Excepting only in rare seasons, one-third of its population is unable to feed the other two-thirds. A deviation of climate so minimum that the United States is but insignificantly affected means a crisis in the Kremlin. Nor is the problem confined to food. The great port, Murmansk, is the Soviet Union's one year-around outlet to the north. But its blessings are secured only by the Gulf Stream's final influence. Should the Arctic ice pack spread south into the Atlantic just enough to shorten the Gulf Stream by a hundred miles or so, Murmansk would no longer be an ice-free port. The rising menace to Murmansk is today being recorded. We have considered the Kuklas' satellite study of the spread of the ice pack in 1972. The condition seems to have worsened. In the summer of 1975 over sixty immense barges headed through the Bering Strait into the Arctic carrying heavy equipment for Alaska's North Slope oil fields. Only a few got through. The Arctic ice pack was reported as the worst in this century. If the trend is continuing—and the report from Alaska is ominous—then in a very few seasons Murmansk could become just another ice-bound Arctic station, and the Soviet Union would be deprived of its only geographically unrestricted outlet to the western world. I take no pleasure in contemplating the explosive political consequences that might result.

I have been discussing climate change largely in terms of cold. But as Britain's Harold Lamb, elder statesman among students of climate, has emphasized throughout all his career, deterioration may be expressed in far more ways than local cooling. Any spread of cold from the poles towards the equator has the effect of increasing the disparity—what is usually called steepening the gradient—between climate belts. Variability of inexplicable order is what we first witness. Ocean currents may shift, and for no apparent reason certain species of fish may vanish from old-time haunts. Abnormal heat may be as much a symptom in one region as abnormal cold in another. What is happening under the pressure of the steepening gradient is a shifting about of those wind currents that we so take for granted. There is the example of the prevailing westerlies, when ten thousand years ago the massive Arctic cold so abruptly relaxed, the last ice sheet withdrew, and the westerlies shifted their moist, moderating attention northward leaving the green Sahara to become what it is today, while bringing to Europe the benevolence of rains and forests, all in a few centuries. Yet of course it is not only the prevailing westerlies, but in lower latitudes the trade winds and the monsoons. Any changes—and all lie beyond our present powers of prediction—can mean floods here, droughts there. And few would be of disastrous significance were it not that we have too many people.

There is an excellent study made by Mitchell concerning rainfall at various stations in northwest India before and after 1920, all dependent on the monsoons. Before that date, throughout a period which we may regard as approximately normal, a dry year with less than half of expected rainfall had the probability of occurring every 8.6 years. From 1920 to 1960, our illusory period which we have come to regard as normal, the weather so improved that the chances of a bad year fell to one in 14. I need not comment on what happened to India's population in those forty years. But one may fairly ask, what happens to the Indian population if since 1960 the rains have merely been returning to normal? We need not ask what has happened to the peoples of the Sahel, just below the Sahara.

As I find it understandable that the Soviet Union could not know what lay ahead when the virgin lands were planted, so I find it just as understandable that what is happening to our climate is a matter of controversy today. We know so little, and all is happening so fast. Nevertheless, a minimum reading of recorded history—let alone a minimum understanding of the Ice Age—would to my mind render many an argument sophomoric.

I think, for example, of a position being taken by certain reputable scientists that can conceivably be founded on nothing but fashionable contemporary thought. There are those who publish their views that the industrial pollution of our atmosphere plays a significant role. The argument makes no sense to me. The increased burning of fossil fuels contributes carbon dioxide to the atmosphere, resulting in what is known as "the greenhouse effect." Were the rise significant on a global scale (which it is not) we should have a rise, not fall, in world temperatures, leading perhaps to a melting of the ice caps. With a single exception such a warming is notably absent in the records of our weather stations. The exception is New Zealand, a land as isolated from industrial pollution as one is apt to find. Nor can the New Zealand experience be typical of the Southern Hemisphere, as the Brazilian would be the first to confirm. His frost-of-the-century in mid-1975 not only destroyed his coming coffee crops but left much of the world's largest coffee plantations in ruins. However fashionable blaming industry may be in our time, I find the argument wanting. I far prefer the consensus of the Brown meeting: we suffered climatic crashes long before smokestacks, and whatever may be industry's many-splendored sins, what happened to the Danes in the thirteenth century cannot have been somebody's fault.

Bryson not only accepts the thesis of rapid climate change but takes the extreme position that such changes are apt to take place in a single century, with the effects spread over a few more by the conservative residue of heat or cold held by the lands or the oceans. He discounts, however, the Kuklas' study of albedo, which I find most persuasive. Albedo is the reflection of sunlight from the earth's surface with consequent loss of heat. Calm ocean reflects back only 5–10 percent, vegetated ground perhaps 15–20 percent. But pack ice and snow fields act as a mirror, returning to interplanetary space about 80 percent of sunlight, with almost total heat loss. If one thinks it over, one can glimpse a chain reaction of sorts. Two or three winters such as that of 1972 so increase the albedo and so decrease our heat absorption that more such winters rise to high likelihood. And so ice sheets are born.

There will be other arguments, since we know so little. There will be the parochial fallacy: in a given season we in America may enjoy bumper crops, while the Soviet Union is devastated by drought, western Europe by heat, Brazil by frost. Our principal anxiety will be the rise in food prices. And there is the public-statement fallacy. The individual scientist may climb out on a limb, but institutions dislike taking chances. And so we receive in the public press soothing statements from departments of agriculture, world food organizations, even highly placed government meteorologists. Beyond the natural inhibitions of a bureaucracy, what the reader of the public press must keep tolerantly in mind is our specialization of experts. The authority on crops, or on weather for that matter, is unlikely to be an authority on Ice Ages.

I can understand much, as I can forgive much. What I can forgive only with strenuous effort, however, is the report by a special panel of our most respected scientific group, the National Science Foundation. Cited uncritically by an agronomist, L. M. Thompson, what was known as the Ad Hoc Panel on the Present Interglacial issued its report in August, 1974. A minor sin was its endorsement of the pollution thesis. Even though our burning of fossil fuels adds only .2 percent annually to the carbon dioxide in our atmosphere—and in the unlikely event that we continued to burn them at the present rate for the next half century, still by then the greenhouse effect would have raised global temperature by a mere one-half of one degree Fahrenheit—yet the panel could state that human activities would tend to prolong the present interglacial. But I save my wrath for the following excursion into know-nothing science:

> The probability of occurrence of a transition associated with the fundamental 100,000 year glacial-interglacial vacillation is about .002 in the next hundred years, and .02 in the next 1000 years.

The hundred-thousand-year cycle is a fiction. The probabilities cited are based on the firm expectation that our interglacial will endure for fifty thousand years, one-half of the fictitious cycle. There is no older trick in the scientific repertory than to present exact statistical deductions to divert our attention from an untenable premise. Not even the old-time seat-of-the-pants geologists, like A. Penck and E. Brückner, who pioneered our studies of the Ice Age, found such regular comings and goings of glaciers. It is true that when in 1961 my wife drew her chart of the Ice Age in *African Genesis,* we estimated on the best evidence then prevailing that the last interglacial had endured for about fifty thousand years. But if an *ad hoc* committee of the National Science Foundation is using *African Genesis* for its scripture, then heaven help us all. Without absolute dating, without a host of new techniques available to the present student of the Ice Age, what we accepted in 1961 was little more than conventional wisdom. The last interglacial, for example, (called Riss-Würm by European geologists) may have been introduced by the very warm period recorded at Hawaii that, as we have seen, quickly deteriorated. And we have now not only sea levels to guide us. The varying temperature of ancient seas is being revealed by the nature of microscopic life found fossilized in deep-sea cores, a study pioneered by technique, developed largely by Emiliani, measures temperature according to the prevalence of an isotope of oxygen in water. Frozen, as in the Greenland or Antarctic ice caps, the record is imperishable. And that is how we know from Greenland of the frightening drop in temperature that occurred in the very midst of the Riss-Würm interglacial. What the geologist faces first is the probability that a considerable advance in ice may have left a record that a succeeding major advance has wiped out; and second, that if a time of great cold did not coincide with a time of heavy winter snow, there Columbia University's Lamont Observatory. A correlating may have been no glaciation at all. Massive evidences point to the Ice Age as a time of large and relatively rapid change. And if the evidences are available to me, then I must assume that they are available to the National Science Foundation.

We are being deceived. Whether the deception arises from mere carelessness, hasty conference, or the mediocre amalgam of opposing viewpoints, the statement of such an august scientific body becomes less than entertaining in a time such as ours. Yet even worse than its callousness when misery hovers is the support it lends to those who care about misery not at all.

I could discover in myself neither tolerance, understand-

199

ing, nor the least measure of forgiveness for the opportunism of political and religious leaders who met in Bucharest and Rome during 1974. The claim was advanced by such unlikely colleagues as Pekin and the Holy See that the population explosion is a myth, and that population control is a genocidal plot on the part of the "imperialist powers" to reduce the numbers of the impoverished countries for whom the rich would be otherwise responsible. Well, when again and again the monsoons fail, and again and again the great temperate fields of wheat and maize and barley and soybeans shrink before the onslaughts of sodden springtimes, early frosts, unprecedented droughts, and inexplicable floods, then we shall have some dark monuments to commemorate yesterday's obscenities, as we dig mass graves.

Changes of climate move in no straight lines, and a good crop or two will wipe away temporary fears. Yet when self-delusion and opportunism become luxuries that can no longer be afforded, then a bit late we shall see ourselves in long perspective. The cultural animal has fallen into a biological trap. Ten thousand years ago we initiated the production of food and people in such quantity that we could never again return to the hunting way. In the past few centuries our unrestricted breeding, combined with falling mortality rates, have produced such a global population that can be supported even by plant foods only in the best and most abnormal of times. And there is only one way back—starvation, decimation, death. The prospect is most unpleasant.

If *Homo sapiens sapiens,* that able but vulnerable little hunter who once stumbled out of his tundra and grasslands to create munificent fields and pastures, could delude himself that he was the master of nature—if this increasingly civilized being, perhaps out of some profound intuition or perhaps out of feeling a bit nervous about it all, invented an all-powerful personal God, then I cannot blame him. I can only wish that he had invented a God better informed about the nature of the Ice Age.

There was once a popular interpretation of modern races as of ancient and independent origin who arrived in our time along separate evolutionary paths. Like most authorities I regard the interpretation as untenable; we differ too little. I have already suggested my own view that when, about 35,000 years ago, we had a breathing spell in the great Würm glaciation and Cro-Magnon man was free to enter western Europe, other branches of the basic *sapiens sapiens* were spreading over all of the Old World from Africa to farthest Asia. There they were checked again by the revived ice sheets until, with the great melt, a people now distinctively Mongolian could penetrate the Americas and give us the last of the separate races, the American Indian.

Wherever we went we made our trivial but necessary adaptations to differing environmental demands. The white skin, lethal baggage in the sun-smitten tropics, admitted larger doses of the northern latitudes' weak ultraviolet rays to produce our necessary Vitamin D. Through a remarkable adaptation, it retained a capacity to tan when occasion demanded. In tropical areas tan-to-black skins became permaent assets offering protection from the excesses of the tropical sun. Adaptations of a heritable sort could be rapid and sometimes wonderful. In the woodlands of northern New York State and adjacent Canada are the Mohawk Indians, a canoe people. One must speculate that sufficient generations of canoeing placed a heavy selection against those with inadequate balance. Today, long after canoes, no iron-worker can match the Mohawk's skill on high, hazardous construction jobs, yet he has retained from his Mongolian origins an inability as an adult to digest milk.

Differences between peoples may be of a most exotic nature, but it is our likenesses that concern me here. They speak of the recent origin of our evolutionary separation. And when one finds a trait common to all peoples, however remotely separated, then there is justification in believing that it has been inherited from our common mother race. Such, for instance, is our capacity for making fire. Such also is our universal capacity for complex speech, since, as has often been pointed out, there is no such thing, in a people however primitive, as a primitive language. The capacity must have evolved in our older days before we spread out to inhabit the earth.

What interests me in the context of this chapter, however, are two psychic qualities that pervade us all, whatever our illiteracy or our sophistication. The first is an inner need to believe in forces larger and more enduring than oneself. The second is the illusion of central position. And both, I believe, are ineradicable legacies of our hunting days.

The need to believe in omnipotent forces is a very old story. We have seen it formalized in Cro-Magnon times through paintings and totems and shamans. We have seen it ritualized in the cannibalizing of brains by Neanderthal and still earlier evidences of *Homo erectus*. The Hawaiians who roasted and devoured Captain Cook may have done it because they enjoyed his flavor, but in greater likelihood they were partaking of the strange and the great. If any overwhelming conceptual difference exists between the skulls at Choukuotien and the more refined Christian communion, in which symbolically we partake of the flesh and blood of Christ, then the difference escapes me.

In the hazardous history of the human being, whether we go out on the hunt or go forth to battle, there has been the mounting sense of our mortal vulnerability. We have needed whatever irrational reinforcements we could find to bolster our confidence. The formalized religions that spread in the larger agricultural communities provided a social reinforcement as well. Strangers we might be, but we bowed to the same gods, and so to an extent, at least, we might trust one another. The religion did not matter too much, whether that of Baal or the class struggle, so long as it united us.

I say that a need to believe in forces larger than ourselves is a very old story, but this cannot be said of the illusion of central position. A quick appraisal might inform us that the two are contradictory. They are not. They reinforce each other.

Central position is the illusion that I am the center of all things. I briefly introduced the concept in *African Genesis* with a broad indication that the idea was not to be taken too seriously. And it was not. But after fifteen more years of observation and pondering, I have concluded that the illusion provides the central dynamic for our kind. No understanding of war or terror, artistic triumph or scientific genius, the most depraved of brutalities or the most exalting of utopian ambitions, can be brought together without a comprehension of this most unique of human qualities answering the question, Why is man man? And no understanding of the whole problem of interglacial man can be approached without further exploration.

In 1961 I described the illusion in terms a bit different from those I would use today. I saw it as originating with the newborn infant's response to a world about him which seemed to exist for his purposes. Breasts or bottles, faces or toys—all attention seems on him alone. Before long he will encounter disillusionment. Whether wetness or hunger, temporary neglect will enlist his rage. He will be appeased. Then comes the baby sister, and the world's attention is diverted. Reality destroys a segment of his central illusion, and he will either accept reality, reorganize his illusion on a more tolerant level, and progress towards maturity, or he will reject it, cling to his total illusion, and move towards neurosis, autistic rejection of reality, perhaps a drug-soaked adolescence enhancing the values of his inner world, or even triumphantly into paranoia. The paranoid accepts reality but interprets unpleasant reality as a world conspiracy of forces allied against himself. Central position is ingeniously affirmed.

My 1961 interpretation was quasi-Freudian, since it examined the illusion in terms of life experience, and must be modified. But there was also a conclusion that bears no revision, and it is a paradox. Without the final illusion, we should be lost. Were we to take the final step of rational disillusionment, and see each of us as one of 3.5 billion human beings swarming about our planet; our planet as a mere chip of rock revolving about a minor star; the sun, our star, an average worker in a galaxy of hundreds of billions of other antlike suns; our galaxy as just one of an infinite number of clusters inhabiting infinite universal space—if our rationality could and should inform us concerning our relation to space, then surely I should not be writing this book. The futility of individual existence would overwhelm me as it would overwhelm you. The indefensibly irrational illusion of central position presses us to get out of bed in the morning to shave or do our make-up, but get on with the day's work. Without it we should die as individuals, become extinct as a species.

I have no more quarrel with the final paradox than when I presented it in 1961. Without the illusion, our nine thousand million cerebral neurons would be no more than disorganized stardust. But two reservations have come about in my later thinking. Many a later study of infants, whether of humans or of other primates, has revealed the helplessness of the young and the trauma that comes with separation from the mother. The observations of Robert Hinde and Thelma Rowell at Cambridge, of Harry and Margaret Harlow at Wisconsin, of James Bowlby, of Goodall and her orphaned chimps, do not square with a built-in illusion. And there is another reservation, for the illusion as we find it must be ascribed not only to the individual but to the social group as well. Where is the band, the clan, the tribe, the nation, or the social class that does not to greater or less degree regard itself as unique and deserving of special attention in the world's transactions?

The social illusion, just as the individual's, may move forward toward maturity, toward recognition of the necessities of competing groups, toward compromise and treaties, toward an enhancement of social identity and larger human harmonies as well, without ever surrendering the dynamics of a central conviction. Or it may retreat into apathy, into the fellowship of helplessness, into compensating convictions of inward superiority, and descend toward extinction. But the illusion may turn as well to social paranoia, about which we know so little, so that with cunning and violence the group directs its rages against the conspiracy of peoples who fail to recognize its central claims.

So it may be that what seems an insanely small group of a dozen or twenty or a hundred individuals may with desperate dedication seek to force on all human populations acceptance of the group's illusion. Or it may just as well be that a nation of fifty million, equally united by a shared conviction of superiority, may go on a rampage of violence to gain mastery over all mankind, for mankind's good. Rare is the social illusion that does not draw from the brain's obedient circuitries rational justifications for the most terrible of transgressions. Rare is the sword without its Bible.

Why do we behave as we do? Why should rational processes be not enough? Well, I can hear the protests of those who assert that the illusion is a fiction, and that rationality would be enough if all could be as rational as they. But just as they deny the reality of history and experience, so they reveal unwittingly their own illusion of central position. And we need not rest with the rationalists, for I can hear the murmur of the convinced Christian, or the convinced Moslem—"If only all the world were Christian, or Moslem." I have already suggested that religion and central position neatly reinforce each other. So likewise do the newer secular religions, such as all the conflicting sects stemming out of Marx and Rousseau. They have the disadvantage of pretending to a rationality subject to proof. The old-time religions, making no such pretense, rested on more irrefragable rocks.

There are two explanations for a human behavior so peculiar, and perhaps they blend. The first, of simple order, is that the human brain is so new, in evolutionary terms, that it has not as yet through natural selection perfected its circuitries. Arthur Koestler regards this deficiency as an error. We got hooked up wrong. I disagree, with greater hope. When it comes to brains we are *nouveaux*. With his *Sociobiology*, Harvard's dynamic E. O. Wilson has published a massive, controversial masterpiece that could easily found a new science. In his book he suggests that, granted time to evolve, granted in evolutionary terms a relatively short time, the human being may encounter the selective necessity of proceeding towards higher levels of altruistic control, which in my own terms would mean an easing of the ferocity of central position. But the second explanation, that our total brain is not all that new, leads me into an area perhaps more pessimistic than Koestler's. We are hooked by an evolutionary heritage far older than the kinks in the new brain.

In earlier books, and with some reference in this one, I have reviewed the subject of animal xenophobia, the social rejection of strangers. I have described it here in terms of chimpanzee avoidance. When we forswore the forest and committed ourselves to the hunting life, we lived in small bands that could only have been widely separated. The territorial command to maintain an exclusive range reasserted a rigor that the fruit-eating ape found unnecessary. The geographical separation of hunting territories meant that we did not often see each other. We had our necessary contacts with other groups for the balanced trading or kidnaping of girls and boys for breeding purposes. Beyond such exchanges, which affected the experience of the whole band not at all, the world of our hunting territory was the only world we knew. Whatever logical capacities our small brains possessed—and they were probably considerable—logic would direct us to conclude that the world of our perceptions was *the* world, and that the members of our little society whom we knew so intimately were *the* people.

Throughout the millions of years of our hunting experience, central position was no illusion at all but reality itself. I have commented on the evidence that Cro-Magnon hunting bands seemed capable of cooperative action when dealing with difficult game like the mammoth or wild horse, but the fossil sites are few. The occasions were probably rare. Small-brained or large-brained, we retained the same essential social isolation dictated by the dispersal of our prey. Then, in shortest order, we encountered fields, flocks, and enlarging sedentary communities. It was an experience for which we were biologically unprepared.

We entered a world of strangers. Our facility for social bonds might increase—a little. The rising powers of priests and landlords and warlords might find means of uniting us in larger groups to serve their ends, but never to this day through a power other than the illusion of central position. For what had been a rational enough phenomenon in our hunting experience became the most irrational of illusions in a time of rising numbers, broadening experience, the adventure of cities, the accumulating kitchen-midden of civilization.

It is an evolutionary explanation, and not necessarily the only one. The neurophysiological explanation—that our brain in the end expanded so fast that it remains yet inoperable without this primitive limitation—only serves to reinforce the social explanation. There may be innumerable considerations, any of them more or less true. They do not alter the demonstrable fact that weak or powerful, pacific or predatory, mature or distorted, the illusion is common to all humanity.

Though it may be the death of us, I cannot conceive of the human being, manipulated perhaps by chemists or utopian magicians so that he loses this supreme irrationality, long remaining a human being. The illusion may inspire the bickerings of husband and wife, the rebellions of children, the quarrels of neighbors, the suicidal ambitions of social groups, the destruction of nations, the death of old gods or the birth of new. But it has likewise been the demon to drive the artist, the inventor, the scientist, the most creative statesman, none of whom made their ventures of value without a somewhat insane conviction of their own rightness. We may turn to the conquerors and the despots, whether a Stalin or a Rameses II, an Alexander, a Napoleon, a Hitler, an "I, Darius, King of Kings," or the smallest-time demagogue in the United Nations Assembly. But there have been others. Perhaps no man in history ever so embraced the illusion of central position as did Jesus Christ, or succeeded for quite so long in persuading quite so many other people that his was not an illusion.

Central position is something uniquely human, something like running feet that we do not share with the chimpanzee, and we must live with it. I must have it if I am to finish this book. You must have it if you are to read my book, since it consists of nothing but one man's view of our history and fate. Neither you nor I could find life endurable if with total rationality we had to face the whole of it. Eugene O'Neill, America's greatest if most pessimistic playwright, concluded that life without illusion is impossible. Like Tiger and Fox, wondering whether the agricultural revolution was indeed quite the cultural advance that we have believed, he could be right.

Rationality is a power that we can never forsake, or we are lost. I am an interglacial man. My rational powers inform me that in two decades, in two centuries, or two thousand years from now—is there a difference?—we shall again be the hosts of ice. Yet though I know it to be true beyond small statistical improbability, still something in me rejects it and refuses to believe. I can no more accept the inevitabilities of nature than Cro-Magnon man at Lascaux, had he been informed, could have accepted the inevitability that within a very few thousand years his hunting world would be gone.

We are a hunting being with a much-too-short experience with that new industry, managing a brain so large, and a still shorter apprenticeship in the fields and the pastures and the workshops of civilization. So what supports me? Well, the illusion that I am different, that you are different, that our kind is different: and that such things cannot happen to us. Even so, it is my rational obligation to press on, and to wonder.

I must wonder what will happen when a deteriorating climate, a shrinking food supply, a starving, still proliferating population, and all our varied illusions of central position, meet one night on a stormy street corner.

There is a question concerning altruism that must concern us now, since it must mightily concern us at some turbulent future date. Just how willingly does one human being sacrifice his own interests for the good of others? Strict Darwinian thought says never—excepting in terms of reproduction. The mother, and even the father on occasion, will boast genetic equipment necessary for the survival of the next generation. But beyond that, forget it.

I was unconvinced. In *The Territorial Imperative,* as I have mentioned, I emphasized the concept which I termed the *amity-enmity complex*. Natural amity exists, but it is not too dependable a commodity in a world of living beings. When adults face a common enemy, however, amity is generated at a rate approximately equal to threat, and altruism flourishes. My argument did not go down too well with those followers of the Rousseau tradition who presume that generosity, amiability, goodness are all portions of our primal endowment. (Whether these people have ever read history or raised a few children, still bewilders me.) Perhaps biologists read more history, raised more children, or more easily recognized that my statement was nothing more than a very old idea presented in a biological context. On the whole they found the amity-enmity complex as a generator of altruism quite in accord with Darwinian devotion to self-interest. But then, in *The Social Contract,* I moved on to the *genetic* fixation of altruistic traits and found many a biologist moving rapidly towards my throat.

Group selection is a subject of as hot debate as any that exists in biology today. Its relation to altruism is plain. If competition takes place not only between individuals but between groups, then the group with greater endowments of loyalty, cooperation, self-sacrifice, and altruism concerning social partners will be selection's survivor. Both Darwin and Wallace foresaw the possibility over a century ago. My own reflections on the long evolution of our hunting bands and interdependent societies led me to conclude that in the millions of passing years some tendency for altruism must have become part of our surviving gene pools. The threatened chimpanzee may take arboreal refuge before even alerting his fellows to danger. In our terrestrial life, existing as prey as well as predator, we could not. As a group we lived or died according to the willingness of individual males or females to accept risk, injury, possible death.

Natural selection, however, poses a sticky problem. Would not the most altruistic of social partners suffer the highest rate of death and disability, therefore leaving fewest descendants—while those most devoted to personal survival leave the most? How could an altruistic gene become part of the descendant gene pool? Population geneticists came up with a variety of dense equations, which I doubt that the reader would find entertaining at this point in my narrative. But then, in the 1960's, sponsored largely by W. D. Hamilton, came an alternative concept: kin-selection. In a small group there tends to be a sharing of genes derived from a common ancestor. A father bequeaths half of his genes to each of his sons. Brothers and sisters carry a half-load of similar genes derived from each parent. The death of a heroic brother does not mean the end of the genetic line, so that an altruistic inheritance becomes possible.

Kin-selection is today widely accepted. I resisted it for a while, reflecting on animal examples in which kinship could scarcely be close enough to explain the acceptance of risk by courageous baboons or unthinking gazelles. Yet such problems could be left to the geneticists. Mine was the problem of human evolution in small, discrete bands in which the leadership of brothers would be a normal event and closeness of genetic relationship all but unavoidable. Altruism there must have been, and kin-selection could explain it. But for contemporary optimists the Israeli geneticist I. Eshel provided a worrisome thought. Such may have been the case in our hunting days, but what would happen to altruism when sedentary times came along, populations enlarged, mixed peoples moved to towns, and emigration to better lands and farther fields diluted or demolished the old close kinship?

I still held fast to my own thought, despite Eshel's thought, that some minimum altruistic tendency generated in our hunting days must still remain in our genetic equipment. But then came a book.

In 1972 Colin Turnbull published *The Mountain People.*

Turnbull is among the most able of American anthropologists. His perceptive study of the Pygmy in the deep Congo forest, published in an earlier book called *The Forest People,* had not only made his reputation but inspired him to study a hunting society living under radically different environmental conditions. He chose the Ik, a people never before studied, who live in the mountains of northeastern Uganda. So little did science know of them that we even had their name wrong and called them *Teuso*. And as Turnbull was to discover we were wrong about their hunting, for they no longer hunted.

Earlier on, it had been different. So long as *sapiens sapiens* had inhabited the area, the Ik (pronounced *Eek*) probably dwelt and hunted in these mountains. Like certain Pygmies they had been net-hunters. It is a technique demanding that the whole society hold a widespread net while drivers press the game into the trap. The cooperative demand resembles far more the old-time days of the hunting band with hand-held weapons than do our more individualistic hunting peoples with their blow-pipe, spear, or bow and arrow. But a tragedy had befallen the Ik. The independent Uganda government had designated their hunting territory as a game reserve where hunting was forbidden. Deprived of their age-old way and the society based upon it, the Ik as individuals fell to pieces. That is how things were when Turnbull arrived.

The Mountain People is a scientific book without a footnote, a straightforward account told by a sophisticated, objective, and most compassionate observer. And it is the most ghastly testament ever to have emerged from the human sciences. Read even on its most superficial level, the book records what hunger—and this must concern us—can do to people.

When Turnbull arrived, the Ik, spread about in their small, stockaded villages, were a hungry lot. They had been denied their ancient hunting way. The government had furnished them with seeds, and a few instructions concerning the planting and care of crops. Hunters do not take easily to the farming discipline. The Ik were indifferent. Besides, there was a drought, and what little effort they expended was largely wasted. It was man against man, husband against wife, parents against children. If an altruistic gene exists in humanity, the Ik failed to demonstrate it. Turnbull writes that he can be grateful to the Ik that they treated him no worse than they treated each other.

But the author presented more drastic conclusions. Regarding the family, he records, "The Ik seem to tell us that the family is not such a fundamental unit as we usually suppose. . . . Children are useless appendages, like old parents. Anyone who cannot take care of himself is a burden and hazard to others." They regard family ties as insane. "The other quality of life that we hold to be necessary, love, the Ik dismiss as idiotic and highly dangerous."

Gone too, to the incredulity of any primate student, is even the bond between mother and child. Nevertheless I recalled the late Professor C. R. Carpenter's experience with some 350 rhesus monkeys that he was transporting from India to form a colony on an island off Puerto Rico. This was before World War II, when Carpenter, alone in the scientific world, was making the earliest observation of primates in a state of nature. The idea of a colony (so successful that it is a principal object of study still) was to establish in semiwild conditions a habitat where the monkeys could be observed under laboratory conditions. On the ship providing the transport, however, there was a necessity to habituate his subjects to new foods, and to do this he had to keep them hungry. Turnbull's exposure to a philosophy of hunger was an accident. So was Carpenter's when, to his horror, he had to observe on the long sea voyage what happened to individual rhesus monkeys when the exigencies of transportation destroyed their natural societies. Hungry mothers not only neglected their young but tore food away from them. At the end of the voyage there were ten dead infants.

Turnbull's experience was comparable to Carpenter's. The Ik mother nurses her child for three years, then throws it out. The toddling child will join its peers in a scavenging existence. Among many another horror story, he writes of a nursing mother who put down her infant beside a water hole where a leopard snatched it and made off. "She was delighted. She was rid of the child and no longer had to carry it about and feed it, and still further it meant that a leopard was in the vicinity and would be sleeping off his dinner and thus an easy kill." She was right. The men found the sleeping leopard, killed it, cooked it, and ate it—semi-digested child and all.

Yet somehow it was not just a matter of hunger. There was the mother whose crawling infant approached closer and closer to the village fire. The men watched in silent suspense. When the infant got burned and screamed, the men erupted in laughter. Pleased, she retrieved her child who had so amused the men.

Hunger was bad enough, and most critics seized on it to illustrate what could happen to a people so deprived. But there was a deeper level of degradation brought home by what I might call the third act, largely ignored by critics. Turnbull returned to the Ik when the droughts were over, when their crops flourished, when rotting tomatoes and pumpkins hung from the village stockades, and baboons consumed the ripening maize. But the Ik, if possible, were worse than ever. Now government relief was available at an aid station some miles distant. Those from the mountain villages who went to fetch it had their stopping places along the road back, where they ate till they vomited, moved on, stopped, ate till they vomited. The objective was to have as little possible left for their return, when they would be forced to share.

It was a Hobbesian world of Everyman against Everyman, from which Hobbes deduced the necessity for the all-powerful state. It is a concept that I have eternally rejected, for excellent reason. In animal societies nothing like the Ik experience could have occurred. While rejecting the stranger, animals look after their own. But Turnbull in the course of his book broods on the possibility that self-delusion is the only truly unique human quality. He presents his conclusion: "The Ik teach us that our much vaunted human values are not inherent in humanity at all, but are associated only with a particular form of survival that we call society, and that all, even society itself, can be dispensed with."

Colin Turnbull is an honest dealer, and his descent into a particular human inferno presents us in the course of his book with a gallery of horrors that no honest reader can deny. But neither can the honest reader deny that we are inspecting just one small fraction of humanity, facing special circumstances, and that to build vast conclusions concerning man's fate on a base so small is quite as absurd as, in more romantic vein, to discover a peaceful, gentle, non-aggressive straggler in a Philippine forest and to hail him as the Noble Savage, primordial man. Nevertheless, warning signals must again flash. The special circumstances of the Ik might at some future date be not so special. The loss of a social tradition—in their case as a consequence of the loss of the hunting way with all its excitement, its ordained routines, its compulsory cooperation, its dangers, its failures, its triumphs—is a loss that could befall us all. For the Ik, Colin Turnbull predicts certain extinction.

Interglacial man faces not a few possibilities. When decimation comes our way, through natural selection we may find a sorting of the peoples. We vary. And there may be those in which, unlike the Ik, a streak of inherent altruism has developed. Or perhaps in weak measure the streak is universal but cannot assert itself without an encouraging social milieu. Again, perhaps our problem of survival in times of desperate circumstances relates little to inherent altruism as such, but much more directly to our effective social mind, to the strength of our social will, and to a delicate balance between our respect for innovation and our long-habituated social traditions. Whatever the quality of our catastrophe, these would be the survivors. It is a pity that any glance about our precatastrophe world reveals such qualities of survival so seldom in the ascendancy.

Yet the modern evolutionist is a persistent optimist. I have discussed the tendency with such noted evolutionists as Konrad Lorenz and the late Louis Leakey. Is it because we take such a long view of time? Is it because we have witnessed such patience, such powers, such ingenuities of survival in life's long history—powers that go beyond any rational explanation? Or is it an appreciation of Lorenz's famous witticism that man as we know him is simply the halfway house between the ape and the human being?

We are not the last station on the line. Over three billion years have passed since living organisms began to take form on our earth. It is two-thirds as long as the history of the planet itself. An unbroken chain of life connects those swampy beginnings with your presence on earth and mine. There have been calamities and extinctions as one line or another failed to adapt to environment and went into natural selection's discard. Had it happened to just one generation in the line that reaches down to us, we should not be wondering about the fate of men, since there would be none.

The rationalist sometimes accuses the evolutionist of substituting Nature for God. It is an oversimplification. Never would the evolutionist bow his head and murmur, "Nature's will." Never would he look on nature as the creative force, but only on life, that single portion of the natural world. Yet there is a small seed of truth in the accusation, for the evo-

216

lutionist gains faith from his contemplations. I know of few rationalists who, placing their hopes on the omnipotent human brain, find much encouragement in our bewildered time.

The story of evolution, despite all of its failures and extinctions, is one of most improbable success. In this narrative we have watched the human experience, as closely as I can guess it, and many a chapter like the African drought has presented an environmental nightmare. Yet enough of us survived to reassemble our genes, temporarily perfect a still more able animal, and tackle another of nature's nightmares, the successive waves of the Ice Age.

Our interglacial experience has been just one more test that accident has thrown our way. I cannot regard our immense cultural conquest of food supply—despite its horrendous biological consequences leading inevitably to a gruesome population outcome—as anything but necessary in the long evolution of Lorenz's human-being-to-be. We failed the test, it is true. We drew from our brief experience with benevolence small philosophies other than indulgence— hedonism, gross materialism and institutionalized injustice; entertainments such as mass slaughter, massive destruction, massive reproduction—and of course hubris and the delusion that we were masters of nature. Faced now by a ruthless future we may, through our greed and our quarrels and our scrambles, take the easy way out and most decisively blow ourselves up. Every logic would support the probability.

Yet I find the proposition dubious. Were we beings without history, were we dependent on nothing but rationality and conditioned learning, my pessimism would be fathomless. But we do have our history, and it is older than the hominid, older than the ape or monkey, older than the tiny arboreal mammals of a hundred million years ago. It is older than the reptiles who bore them, older than the first air-breathing fish, as old as those first microscopic organisms, in our earth's young years, who perfected before all others a determination to survive.

There will be those of us of rare courage and endowment that will accept, perhaps welcome, certainly adapt to a new kind of icy world—which in truth is a very old kind of world that we have long survived before. I doubt that they will remember interglacial man as harshly as we sometimes see ourselves. The beauty that Cro-Magnon invented, we took to soaring heights of sounds and words and spires. Perhaps a few shrines will remain, in the valley of the Nile or on a warm Sicilian shore, and they will visit them as we once visited the caves of the Dordogne. They may rightly guess that a past race that so loved beauty in fortunate circumstances may have loved each other.

They will keep much of value that we created, while discarding most as baggage that the new bad-weather animal cannot afford. There will be the art of cooking, and certain seeds to help them along in their few favorable climates and poor tropical soils. There will be old books which they will read with amusement and wonder at the way we were, until they come to seem too heavy to be worth lugging about—or until, more likely, the pages disintegrate. In the meantime, however, it would be a curious inheritance from all our technological paraphernalia if the one compulsory artifact remained eyeglasses. Evolution had never had the opportunity to encourage eyes fit for reading.

We were truly not too bad a sort—stupid, it is true, much given to self-delusion, and as tempted by sentimentality as by savagery—but on balance an experimental being who, while so often doing his worst, not too infrequently did his best. Though we weren't too strong about morality, still we thought quite a bit about it and could feel guilty once in a while. Though genetic altruism may have eluded us, still we were always preaching it in anticipation of a glowing collection plate. (And there were always those few, let us not forget, who weren't that concerned about the collection plate.) And there was this idea of education. While normally it consisted of the most callous brainwashing, still it was an idea that some future people could make use of.

What I must suspect is that the survivors of this glacial calamity that will befall us, decimate us, and through most appalling natural selection discard the Ardreys with their paunch bellies, bad knees, flat feet—will pool their collective genes into one more subspecies of *Homo sapiens* in a few tens of millennia, and take one more step away from the ape in the direction of the human being. I suspect that in an infinitely rigorous climate, with eternally hostile environmental demands, their mythology will become more pragmatic, and yet more demanding of belief. As the Greek poets and dramatists went back to Agamemnon and their centuries-old predecessors to whip into the Greek populace what was right, what was wrong, so I suspect that our Ice Age inheritors, whatever their literate capacities, will turn back to the villains and heroes of interglacial man for the lessons of what to do, and what not. It could be our greatest legacy.

As an interglacial man, I feel no embarrassment, except for one thing—that we ended the hunting way. It had shaped us, given us—anatomically and socially—the way we are. But we killed off our fellow species in the natural world. The death of the hunter and the hunted must be the sin that interglacial man committed in the memories of his inheritors. How do you live when the tundra returns but not the reindeer, the aurochs, the extinct mammoth?

Animal species—if they are not truly extinct—have a way of reviving when ecological turns may encourage a return. It isn't just a matter of the human predator. Far more drastic is the land where they may roam without interference from farmers. As farmers must surely decline in number, so may the ecological elbow-room of species. So perhaps—and only perhaps—animal prey may expand to relieve the problem of food supply for that endangered species, future man, and man the hunter may again have his day.

Yet again, I must express my doubt. We shall not have gone back to the bow and arrow, let alone the hand-held weapon. We shall keep, beyond eyeglasses, those technological advances in killing, so that our descendants will never be a portion of animal species on equal terms. The hunter died when he achieved supremacy.

Perhaps the death of the hunter will be the long monument to interglacial man. We denied a future to our successor beings. Evolution will tell us one day whether the balance of nature and evolving man—from the risen ape to the human being—will ever have been restored. I cannot know, nor can you, since we shall all have long been gone.

All I can assert is that I was happy, even proud, to have been a member of interglacial man. We sailed the world and brought back our impressions of San Francisco Bay. We explored the universe of the mind, touched on the moon, demonstrated through our molecular genetics that all life is one, demonstrated through natural selection how life outlives accident. We did so many things that could not have been done without our benevolent interglacial. Now we must retreat as nature resumes its hostility. And were I allowed to live long enough to witness the change—an impossibility at my age—I should find myself nostalgic for the good old interglacial days.

I should miss the opportunity of movement, and the chance, for example, to enter an African kraal and recognize that long before their northern counterparts, these people created compassionate and most realistic welfare states through tribal acceptances. I shall miss wandering along the Seine, or through the corridors of the Uffizi gallery in Florence. I shall miss the overconfident architectural monuments of Piccadilly, and the endless green spread of Seattle's garden homes. I shall miss window-shopping in New York's Madison

Avenue or Rome's Via Condotti, as I shall miss my crabmeat on San Francisco's Fisherman's Wharf. I shall miss so much the happy cry of children as they ride the carousel on a Paris boulevard.

Well, sooner or later it will all be gone. As an interglacial man, I shall regret it. As a risen ape, however, I must have no regret, but rather a warm sort of pride for an ape that has risen so far along the Lorenzian course of becoming a human being. His future rests beyond an icy horizon. We have come this far, and that is about all one can say.

I am haunted by the happy cries of children and the clamor of the calliope.

Bibliographical Comment

In my previous books I presented detailed, point-by-point bibliographies, frequently including references to technical publications not easily available to general readers. In the early years the library shelf devoted to ethology and to human evolution was slim to the point of nonexistence. Now, however, a readily available literature exists, and with the publication of *The Hunting Hypothesis* I have concluded that a supplementary reading list of books available today will be of greater value to the reader. I shall not neglect scientific papers that have entered into my controversial hypothesis, but the principal aim of this bibliography is to acquaint readers with at least a part of the immense literature now obtainable, whether or not in accord with my view. If they care, then they may judge.

First in chronological terms comes Eliot Howard's classic *Territory in Bird Life* (1920), today available everywhere in paperback. Carveth Read's equally classic volume, *Origins of Man* (1925), introduced the hunting hypothesis, but so far as I know it is long out of print. As Professor Fox has commented, you could teach an entire introductory course in anthropology out of that single book. There is a considerable hiatus until the late Sir Julian Huxley's imperishable 1942 volume *Evolution: A Modern Synthesis,* which first explored what we now call ethology but on a broader biological scale established the twentieth-century interpretation of evolution now known as neo-Darwinism. The next important step was the publication in 1951 of Niko Tinbergen's *Study of Instinct,* a book that is difficult to obtain today but that established ethology as a science in its own right. The following year Konrad Lorenz published *King Solomon's Ring,* easily available today but in its time too enchanting for scientists to take seriously.

Historically, these were the classic steps leading up to the 1958 *Behavior and Evolution,* a symposium volume edited by A. Roe and G. G. Simpson, that brought together the most advanced thoughts of the new generation of biologists. From his contribution I have cited S. L. Washburn's early statements of the hunting hypothesis; the book remains compulsory reading even today for any general reader with an interest in contemporary interpretations of evolution. Together with Theodosius Dobzhansky's *Mankind Evolving* (1962) this book attains a climax in the trend initiated by Huxley twenty years earlier.

In the same year S. L. Washburn edited another symposium volume, *The Social Life of Early Man,* which took the first major step along a new pathway, the study of man's evolving past. It had been preceded by two specialized volumes published by the British Museum (Natural History), still definitive and available in inexpensive editions. The first was Kenneth P. Oakley's *Man the Tool-Maker* (1947), the second W. E. Le Gros Clark's *History of the Primates* (1949). I cannot conceive of writing without them. It was from the rich contributions to Washburn's symposium volume, however, that I drew such material as Alberto Blanc's study of Pleistocene rituals, Oakley's history of fire-making, and Vallois's painstaking analysis of Pleistocene life-expectancy. 1962 is a long time ago, in terms of modern study of human evolution, and I remain amazed how few of the book's contributions have been outdated. The Wenner-Gren Foundation, who sponsored the symposium, deserves our thanks. Not until 1965, when Irven DeVore edited another symposium volume, *Primate Behavior,* did anything of comparable quality appear.

The trend of the 1960's—and I shall presume for the remainder of 1970's—has been a proliferation of primate studies all in the direction of a better understanding of our own zoological family, but excited by the East African discoveries of our human and protohuman past. I could cite paper after paper by the Leakey family concerning their East African revelations. For the reader who enjoys technical detail, I recommend Cambridge University Press's publication of an expensive series concerning *Olduvai Gorge,* in particular Louis Leakey's volume 1 (1965), and that of his wife, Mary Leakey: volume 3 (1971). The best summation is that by Sonia Cole—*Leakey's Luck* (1975), a biography.

The attention which students have lavished on monkeys and apes in so many specialized studies is so great that I do not care to list them here. Washburn stated the problem neatly when he said that in 1960, for lack of material you could scarcely teach a course in primate behavior; by 1970, so copious was the material, you could scarcely read it. Out of it all emerged the classic *In the Shadow of Man,* by Jane Goodall, to which I have referred frequently. Dian Fossey, with her study of gorillas, may in the future produce a comparably everlasting work. (I strongly suspect that women are better at this sort of thing than men. Nevertheless, it was a man who initiated such studies.)

In the 1930's C. R. Carpenter published monograph after monograph concerning the behavior of primates in the wild. They were contemporary with the Nobel prizewinners' papers, yet they far exceeded them in terms of truly objective methods of observing animals in an authentic wild state. His papers, however, vanished from print. Fortunately Penn State University has republished them all, in 1964, in a volume called *Naturalistic Behavior of Nonhuman Primates.* It is technical, it is not for every reader, but it is a historical landmark in the progress of modern evolutionary studies.

There came a switch, however, from studies of primates. Apes were not all, as I have emphasized in this book. Our most assiduous student of dangerous animals, George B. Schaller, laid down the law in a paper published with a colleague, G. R. Lowther, in the *Southwestern Journal of Anthropology* in late 1969. (Since he developed his views in following books, the remote reference may not concern us.) From his early paper I described in this book his experience of seeking meat on foot. But just as Washburn's symposium volume shifted our attention from general evolution to human, so Schaller's paper shifted our attention from our primate inheritance to our predatory experience.

Until the publication of his paper in 1969, we had almost no reliable record of the behavior of social predators. Then, from 1970 on, came in rapid succession David Mech's *The Wolf; Innocent Killers,* by Jane Goodall and Hugo van Lawick; Schaller's own definitive volume, *The Serengeti Lion;* and Hans Kruuk's all-important *The Spotted Hyena.*

If, in Schaller's terms, we are to accept the human being as an ape-descended being who through millions of years led an increasingly predatory life, subjected to natural selection in terms of his predatory capacity (the thesis of this book), then we must contemplate both our ape inheritance and our natural selection as predators. While I have been contemplating this thesis since *African Genesis,* now that it has approached a certain scientific respectability the two areas in our literature must receive equal attention.

I cannot neglect in such a bibliography the books of derogation such as Ashley Montagu's *Man and Aggression,* quoting a small host of critics who rarely refrain from quotation out of context, misquotation entire, or the innuendo that we are spending careers of research to prove this political thesis or that. The most prominent of us—Tinbergen, Lorenz, Desmond Morris, Tiger and Fox, and myself—have been the prime targets. And perhaps Konrad Lorenz and I brought it on ourselves in 1966 with the simultaneous publication of *On Aggression* and *The Territorial Imperative*. The sensation introduced the word *ethology* not only to a large public but to dinner-party gossip as well. The literature of derogation seems founded more on gossip than information.

Despite peripheral counter-attacks, the new movement in evolutionary concepts continues to go forward and to broaden. In 1972 another Nobel prizewinner, the French molecular biologist, Jacques Monod, published his *Chance and Necessity*, a book as profound as it is pertinent. Then as recently as June, 1975, came Edward O. Wilson's *Sociobiology: The New Synthesis*. Massive, comprehensive, superbly informed, the book presents either a climax to all the literature that has come before or, more likely in my opinion, the foundation text for a future academic discipline resolving at last the conflicts of the natural and social sciences.

In the meantime solid books concerning human evolution have appeared in number: Bernard Campbell's *Human Evolution* a bit early, in 1967; John Napier's *The Roots of Mankind* (1970); J. Desmond Clark's *The Prehistory of Africa* in the same year; the easily read *Emergence of Man* (1969) by John Pfeiffer, and Herman Wendt's *From Ape to Adam* (1972). I by no means agree with all the conclusions expressed, but at last a literature exists for the reader to judge. Perhaps the best of all is an early one: F. Clark Howell's *Early Man* (1965). It came too soon to describe his own later, astonishing discoveries in the Kenya-Ethiopia Omo Valley, but it is a marvel of clarity, excitement, and common sense.

About 1970, just as the books on the great predators were beginning to come out, the rush of discoveries centered in northwestern Kenya disrupted the library shelf. A few books, because of their preoccupation with far later stages of our history, remain unaffected: Sonia Cole's *The Neolithic Revolution,* for example, another invaluable and inexpensive publication by the British Museum (Natural History), which appears constantly in revised editions; *The Evolution of Man and Society* (1969), by the famous British geneticist C. D. Darlington, whose approach is so controversial as to reduce the arguments of anthropologists to passing mosquito bites; and the continuing series of volumes entitled *Perspectives on Evolution,* edited by S. L. Washburn and Phyllis Dolhinow.

In general, however, the discoveries and controversies that have piled up since 1970 force the reader to turn to the scholarly papers of the time for original source material. To help decipher them, there are older, excellent, and quite technical works: *African Ecology and Human Evolution* (1963), edited by Howell and F. Bourlière, and *Background to Evolution in Africa* (1967), edited by W. W. Bishop and J. D. Clark. Both are records of further Wenner-Gren Foundation symposia. And there is the book without which no student of our fossil past can proceed: Kenneth P. Oakley's *Frameworks for Dating Fossil Man,* first published in 1964 but proceeding through revised editions. For this book there exists no competitor.

Beyond these three works, I must mention two more symposia, each valuable in part. The first was the consequence of a famous symposium at the University of Chicago: *Man the Hunter* (1968), edited by R. Lee and Irven DeVore. It is deeply marred by the "living fossil" fallacy that contemporary hunting peoples, with their fire and their long-distance weapons, offer models for our ancestral way. The other is the Smithsonian's *Man and Beast* (1969). By this date the basic controversy was beginning to take hold, and the book's flaw lies in the occasional failure of participants to state whether they are dealing with science or polemics.

While, as I have stated, I should find it confusing to list

all of the specialized papers and publications that have contributed to my own book, I still find it necessary to give brief but emphatic mention to those that have contributed to any judgment concerning my admittedly controversial hypothesis. Early references appear in my earlier books, but there are many of present importance, and I list them in the approximate order in which they appear in my text.

Martin, Paul. "Pleistocene Overkill." *Natural History* (December, 1967). This is one of numerous papers that Martin has published.

Isaac, Glynn. "The Diet of Early Man." *World Archaeology* (February, 1971).

Kortlandt, Adriaan. "Bipedal Armed Fighting in Chimpanzees." Symposium XVI, Congress of Zoology, Washington, D.C., vol. 3 (1963).

"Protohominid Behavior in Primates." Symposium of Zoological Society, London, no. 10 (August, 1963).

Thorpe, W. H. "Comparison of Vocal Communication in Animals and Men." In *Non-Verbal Communication,* ed. R. A. Hinde. Cambridge: Cambridge University Press, 1972.

Teleki, Geza. "The Omnivorous Chimpanzee." *Scientific American* (January, 1973).

Bygott, J. D. "Cannibalism among Wild Chimpanzees." *Nature* (August 18, 1972).

Simons, E. L. "Late Miocene Hominid from Fort Ternan, Kenya." *Nature* (February 1, 1969).

Leakey, L. S. B. "Bone-Smashing by Late Miocene Hominid." *Nature* (May 11, 1968).

Leakey, Richard. "Further Evidence of Lower Pleistocene Hominids from Lake Rudolf." *Nature* (May 28, 1971). This is one of a series of papers by Richard Leakey giving technical detail concerning his discoveries. They appear almost annually, as do his discoveries.

Bartholomew, George, and Birdsell, J. M. "Ecology and the

Protohominids." *American Anthropologist* (October, 1953). This is a very old paper that I have listed many times in bibliographies, but it is appropriate and has never been refuted.

Hsu, K. J. "When the Mediterranean Dried Up." *Scientific American* (December, 1972). Also in *Nature* (March 23, 1973).

Fleming, J. D. "The State of the Apes." *Psychology Today* (January, 1974).

Linden, E. *Apes, Men and Language*. New York: Saturday Review Press, 1974.

Crawford, Michael, and Crawford, Sheilagh. *What We Eat Today*. London: Spearman, 1972.

Crawford, M. A., and Sinclair, A. J. "Nutritional Influences in the Evolution of the Mammalian Brain." CIBA Foundation Symposium, October, 1971.

Leopold, A. C., and Ardrey, Robert. "Toxic Substances in Plants and the Food Habits of Early Man." *Science* (May 5, 1972).

Bryant, V. M., Jr., and Williams-Dean, G. "The Coprolites of Man." *Scientific American* (January, 1975).

Hess, E. "Attitude and Pupil Size." *Scientific American* (April, 1965). By the same author, *The Tell-Tale Eye*. Von Nostrand Einhold, 1975.

Nishida, T. and Kawanaka, K. "Inter-Unit Group Relations among Wild Chimpanzees." *African Studies*. Kyoto University, 1972.

Cullen, E. "Adaptations in the Kittiwake to Cliff Nesting." *Ibis* (99:275–302, 1957).

Klein, R. G. "Ice-Age Hunters of the Ukraine." *Scientific American* (June, 1974).

Leakey, Richard. "Advanced Plio-Pleistocene Hominid from East Rudolf." *Nature* (April 13, 1973).

Leakey, L. S. B., and Ardrey, Robert. "Man the Killer." *Psychology Today* (September, 1972).

Turnbull, Colin. *The Mountain People*. New York: Simon and Schuster, 1972.

Concerning future world climate, the most important recent references are the following:

BIBLIOGRAPHICAL COMMENT

Bray, J. R. "Glaciation and Solar Activity Since the Fifth Century B.C. and the Solar Cycle." *Nature* (November 16, 1968).

Bryson, R. A. "A Perspective on Climatic Change." *Science* (May 17, 1974).

Johnsen, S. J., et al. "Climatic Oscillations 1200–2000 A.D." *Nature* (August 1, 1970).

Ku Teh-lung, et al. "Eustatic Sea Level 120,000 Years Ago on Oahu, Hawaii." *Science* (March 8, 1974).

Kukla, G. J., and Kukla, H. J. "Increased Surface Albedo in the Northern Hemisphere." *Science* (February 22, 1974).

Kukla, G. J. and Matthews, R. K. "When Will the Present Interglacial End?" The report on the Brown University meeting. *Science* (October 13, 1972).

Thompson, L. M. "Weather Variability, Climatic Change, and Grain Production." *Science* (May 9, 1975).

Wahl, E. W., and Bryson, R. A. "Recent Changes in Atlantic Surface Temperatures." *Nature* (March 6, 1975).

Winstanley, D. "Rainfall Patterns and General Atmospheric Circulation." *Nature* (September 28, 1973).

Index

232

Robert Ardrey

Robert Ardrey was born in Chicago in 1908. He graduated from the University of Chicago, where he began studying the sciences of man. After years as a successful playwright, he returned to the study of man and his origins in 1955, on a visit to Africa. The resulting books, *African Genesis* (1961), *The Territorial Imperative* (1966), and *The Social Contract* (1970), have had an enormous impact, both popular and scientific, and have done much to advance our understanding of man's nature. Mr. Ardrey lives in Rome with his wife, the former Berdine Grunewald.